VOICES OF THE TALENTED TENTH

Values of Young Black Males in Higher Education

Odell Horne, Jr.

University Press of America,® Inc.
Lanham · Boulder · New York · Toronto · Plymouth, UK

Copyright © 2007 by
University Press of America,® Inc.
4501 Forbes Boulevard
Suite 200
Lanham, Maryland 20706
UPA Acquisitions Department (301) 459-3366

Estover Road
Plymouth PL6 7PY
United Kingdom

Library of Congress Control Number: 2006933314
ISBN-13: 978-0-7618-3637-7 (paperback : alk. paper)
ISBN-10: 0-7618-3637-3 (paperback : alk. paper)

Table of Contents

LIST OF TABLES

PREFACE

This study examines the relationship between success and the emotional, psychological and spiritual development of young black males. This study was based on the premise that in order for young black males to be successful in life they have to have a high degree of emotional, psychological and spiritual development.

A descriptive study was utilized to investigate the characteristics of successful young black males in college. Survey and interviews were utilized as the primary data gathering techniques. The researcher found that the young black males who were surveyed and interviewed did have high degree of emotional, psychological and spiritual development.

The conclusions drawn from the findings suggest that the young black males surveyed developed emotionally and psychologically through the positive relationships they have experienced in their lives. While their spiritual development is more indirectly related to the positive relationships they have experienced in their lives, it was through these relationships that they relied on the church for their spiritual development.

Odell Horne, Jr. (Decatur, Georgia)
May 2006

CHAPTER ONE
INTRODUCTION

PURPOSE OF STUDY

Most of the research concerning young black males has dealt with negative, pathological behaviors such as crime, violence, drugs and a variety of other harmful behaviors that have been used to pigeonhole a significant number of this population. Many young black males have internalized the stereotypes that American culture has about them and they have acted upon these stereotypes. These stereotypes include being oversexed, being poor students and having little regard for authority, just to mention a few. In spite of this, many young black males have not accepted the allegations placed upon them, allegations such as they are violent, disrespectful and rude. Rather, they have risen above society's expectations in order to create a better life for themselves and their families. The purpose of this study is to examine the relationship between success and the values that attribute to the personal development of young black males. Specifically, it will focus on what are the values that young black males hold to concerning the emotional, psychological and spiritual dimensions of life that contribute to personal development. Very little research has been done on these factors and how they contribute to the development and the success of young black males. This researcher's pursuit is to contribute to the small, but growing, body of knowledge on young black males, their development and their success. The examination of this topic will not be exhaustive, yet this researcher plans to shed light on some research as it relates to the development of successful young black males.

The values of the emotional dimension reflects the way a person reacts to, handles and approaches situations and circumstances, whether positive or negative, in their lives. The values of the emotional dimension indicate one's maturity or immaturity, peace or pain, fight or flight. The values of the psychological dimension examine how people see life, how they identify them-selves and what they think about themselves and others.[1] The mindset of young black males determines whether they assimilate American cultural standards into their lives or not. It also will help them to set goals they want to achieve. The values of the spiritual dimension examine the belief about those things that people do not have any control. It manifests itself through an indi-vidual's values and belief system. There is very little current research on young black males and their values of the emotional and spiritual dimensions of life; yet, these areas are of vital importance in looking at successful young black men.

FOCUS OF STUDY

According to the 2000 U.S. Census, there are 1.8 million black males be-tween the ages of 18 to 24,[2] of which, 469,000 are enrolled in a college or university.[3] One hundred and twenty-four thousand have an associate degree or higher.[4] The focus of this study will be black males between the ages of 18 and 24 who attend Clark Atlanta University, in order to determine the rela-tionship between their values of the emotional, psychological and spiritual de-velopment and their success.

SIGNIFICANCE OF STUDY

This study gives a voice to successful young black males who are en-rolled in colleges and universities and it challenges the stereotypes of young black males and their lack of success. Some of the young men are the first person in their family to attend college. Some of them grew up in poverty and they knew that the best way to achieve their goals in life was to attend college. In the face of oppression, many young black males have succeeded in various endeavors whether academic, athletic, artistic, technological, or in business.

Included in this study is an analysis of the role the father plays in the be-havioral development of successful young black males. The role of the family will be examined as a contributing factor to the development of successful young black males. For blacks in America spirituality has been a source of stability. An understanding of the spiritual dimension of successful young black males should yield a greater insight into the foundation of their devel-opment. Resiliency is a factor that will be analyzed when dealing with the values of the psychological aspect of developing successful young black males.

RESEARCH QUESTIONS

The research questions are: (1) how does the mastery of certain values of the emotional, psychological and spiritual dimensions of life contribute to the development of successful young black males? (2) What are some of the val-ues that influence the development of successful young black males?

OVERVIEW OF CHAPTERS

Chapter One has introduced the topic of young black males who attend a college or university and some attributes that make them successful. Those attributes include the emotional, psychological and spiritual aspects of life. The significance and focus of this study are discussed.

Chapter Two gives the background of the problems that young black men in America face. This includes examining society's perception of young black males versus the reality of being a young black male. It also discusses the previous work by other researchers in this area. The previous research is evaluated for its strengths and weaknesses, its reliability and validity. The chapter also details the conceptual framework and methodology used to carry out the research.

Chapter Three presents the findings of the research conducted on the emotional values of the Talented Tenth.

Chapter Four presents the findings of the research conducted on the psychological values of the Talented Tenth.

Chapter Five presents the findings of the research conducted on the spiritual values of the Talented Tenth.

Chapter Six concludes the research with the Limitations of the Study.

DEFINITION OF TERMS

Average—a single value that summarizes or represents the general, average to mean what is, or what is perceived to be the norm in society.

Emotional—the response to life's situations, whether good or bad.

Father wound—an emotional void that is caused by the emotional or physical absence of a father in a child's life.

Invisibility—a psychological experience that is caused by racism that has done damage to the psyche of young black males.

Mastery—the possession or display of a skill or technique.

Personal development—the process of maturation that people go through that should move them into adulthood.

Psychological—reflected in the way a person thinks and how he behaves.

Spiritual—religious knowledge is internalized and life decisions are filtered through personal convictions about God.

Successful—indication of those who have achieved or are achieving their goals or following a path that will lead to their betterment as human beings.

Talent—a natural or spiritual gift of an individual that sets him apart from others who attempt to accomplish something through learning or practice.

Talented Tenth—as defined by W.E.B. DuBois, the best and the exceptional men of the race who are developed that they may guide the masses.

Values—principles, standards, or qualities that are deemed desirable by a group or a society.

Young—the early stage of life, having little experience, or recently coming into being. In this work, "young" will refer to young adults, which the U.S. Census Bureau identifies as those between the ages of 18 and 24.

ENDNOTES:

1) Walter A. McCray, *Black Young Adults: How to Reach Them, What to Teach Them* (Black Light Fellowship, 1992), 9.

2) U.S. Census Bureau, Census 2000: Male Population by Age, Race, and Hispanic or Latino origin in the United States: 2000.

3) U.S. Census Bureau, Census 2000: Enrollment Status of the Population 3 years Old and over, by Age, Sex, Race, Hispanic Origin, Nativity, and Selected Educational Characteristics: October 2000.

4) U.S. Census Bureau, Census 2000: Educational Attainment of the Population 15 Years and Over, by Age, Sex, Race, and Hispanic Origin: March 2000.

CHAPTER TWO
CONTEXT OF THE PROBLEM

STATEMENT OF THE PROBLEM

More black women pursue higher education than black men. Much of the research that has been conducted on young black males has focused on negative, "pathological" behavior. The U.S. Department of Education research shows a great disparity between black females and black males in higher education.[1] More than sixty-two percent of black college students are female and they comprise fifty-seven to sixty-six percent of blacks that are awarded a college degree on any level.[2] The percentage of black men attending college between 1984 to 1997 declined from just over forty percent (40.6%) to just under thirty-eight percent (37.4%).[3] Of the 5,043 students who attended Clark Atlanta University in 1995, 1,583 were males (31.4%).[4] These figures remained stable in the fall 2002 semester as 30 percent of the 4,813 students enrolled at Clark Atlanta were males.[5]

CHOOSING CRIME OVER EDUCATION

Many are not attending college because they have chosen to become involved in crime. It is common knowledge that there are more black men involved in the legal system than in college. If a person has been convicted of a drug charge, he cannot receive financial aid, which in turn has hindered many who have collegiate potential, but because of the bad choices he has made in life, he is not able to attend college. Because of poverty, many black males are looking for ways in order to make money and selling drugs allows them to do that. Poverty and frustration, mixed with institutional racism, have been the cause for many to rebel against the system. Criminal activity is a manifestation of this frustration. Anthony E. O. King's research puts the homicide rate for black teenagers at three to five times greater than white teenagers.[6]

ECONOMIC REASONS

Crime and drug involvement have greatly reduced the number of black males who are eligible to attend college. Many academicians believe that black males are also choosing to enter the military, or go to work immediately after high school.[7] One of the reasons may be economic. Some young black males who grew up in poverty may choose to go to work. Many may choose the military because it offers them opportunity for advancement, money for college and skills they may not learn in a college classroom. For those black males who choose to go to work, they are discriminated against more often in "Corporate America" because they are seen as a threat to the white-male management structure,[8] whereas the military gives them a more level playing field where they can show their talent.

FATHER WOUND

The lack of positive black male role models is an acute problem. Many young black males grow up in homes without a father or another positive male role model. Some of those who do have their father in the home may suffer from abuse, or they may have had a father who was emotionally absent. Robert Hill points out that because of the strong achievement orientation of the black family, those who grew up with their father in the home were expected to finish college.[9] Hill argues that the extended kinship network of African–American families has been a buffer against a racist society, for young black males who did not grow up with their fathers.[10] While this is true, the "ongoing war" with the legal system has been the cause of the loss of many young black males to prison.

MEDIA'S PERCEPTION OF YOUNG BLACK MALES

Arguably, the most powerful tool in the war against young black males is the media. The portrayals of black men as athletes and entertainers are some of the few positive images that they see of themselves and are direct reflections of what America thinks of them or in which they have been allowed them to excel. Young black males have, in turn, internalized these images and are perpetuating them.

BACKGROUND OF THE PROBLEM

POOR EDUCATIONAL EXPERIENCE

Kevin Sims, Knight, and Dawes note that young black males receive discipline more often in high school than anyone else.[11] Education is seen as passive and feminine by young black males; couple this with low teacher expectations and many of them are doomed to fail. The cultural gulf that exists between white teachers and black students leads to a misconception of actions, such things as talking aloud without raising their hands, are seen as deviant behavior. Young black males are placed in special education classes, and/or "tracked" more often because of perceived deviant behavior. It is believed that black students learn better in groups and when the focus is on relational issues; this however, is not the curriculum of most public school systems.

The majority of young black males who do graduate from high school and go on to college attend a predominantly white school (85%)[12], as though the cultural values of the educators will change magically because they are in an environment of higher education. Young black males who participated in college athletics had positive levels of social adjustment and self-esteem; however, these factors had a negative correlation on academic achievement.[13]

MORE OF THE FATHER WOUND

H. Elaine Rodney and Mupier acknowledged, "That the father absence...had an apparent negative effect on serious criminal behaviors, alcoholism and occupational achievement. Violent children are 11 times more likely not to live with fathers"[14] The extended family network is invaluable when the father of a young black male is not around to nurture him. The self-esteem of young black males is attached to the relationship with their father, or other positive male role models. The presence of the father, or another positive male role model, in the lives of young black males curtails many behavioral problems. Researchers have also found young black males who grew up in a home without their father experienced significantly more problems regarding conduct disorder. In fact, there were no positive statistics that any researchers were able to discover for those who grew up without their father or another positive male role model. Jay C. Wade goes a step further and acknowledges that some young black males who grow up in father—absent families have problems with sex-role and gender identification.[15] He further purports that those who grew up with a nurturing father are less likely to struggle with issues of sexuality and masculine identity development.[16]

HYPER MASCULINITY

Many young black males have responded to their familial circumstances with "hyper masculinity." Shannette M. Harris states that this redefinition of manhood includes aggressive behavior, disdain for feminine qualities and denial of vulnerability.[17] This is also a reaction to the Eurocentric norms that dominate American society. Another factor in fostering "hyper masculine" behavior is the peer groups. Harris believes that because peer groups meet the needs of belonging and security, young black males are vulnerable to the demands of their peer groups.[18] Thus, developing one's own identity outside of the group is the cause of great strain for many young black males.

INVISIBILITY

Invisibility is an environmental factor that is caused by systematic oppression. Christine J. Yeh proposes, "The negative stereotypes imposed on African-American males contradict their beliefs about who they are, thus creating a state of confusion and bewilderment . . . on the streets, in stores, on elevators and in restaurants we are seen as potential criminals or servants, not as ourselves." [19] Young black males are examples of the "double–consciousness" that DuBois wrote about one hundred years ago. "An American, a Negro; two souls, two thoughts, two unreconciled strivings"[20] These competing roles are not only responsible for how young black males feel, but it also defines who they are in American society. Gail Elizabeth Wyatt believes "that feelings of invisibility can severely impair self-esteem, racial identity development and an individual's personal growth." [21] Some black males have attempted to deny their race in order to gain acceptance as a person; however, this eventually leads to self-hatred. In spite of all the negatives that are associated with being a young black male, Yeh points out some positive responses to invisibility; including a stronger character, resiliency and creativity. [22]

SUICIDE IS ON THE RISE

In recent years, suicide has become one of the biggest problems among young black males. According to the Centers for Disease Control and Prevention in Atlanta, the suicide rate for blacks between the ages of 10 and 19 has more than doubled in the past 20 years, rising from 2.1 per 100,000 in 1980 to 4.5 per 100,000 in 1998. [23] Jewelle T. Gibbs states that black males engage in violent confrontations with the police, their family, or peers in order to precipitate homicide. [24] This is actually an attempt to commit suicide, but because of their belief system, many young black males would not attempt suicide, but may instead put themselves into a position to be killed by someone else. Scholars have not clearly defined the reasons why young black men are committing suicide. The overall violence of American society is certainly a factor in homicide, but it is more logical to believe that societal pressures or oppression are reasons why they are committing suicide.

THE HOMICIDE RATE IS STILL HIGH

Homicide is a leading cause of death for young black males. The homicide rate for young black males was 150–200 murders per 100,000 individuals from 1990–1995, which was more than eight times higher than the homicide rate for young white males. [25] Julie A. Phillips theorizes that the lack of social controls, structural discrimination and choices are the factors that contribute to the high homicide rate among young black males. [26] Phillips believes that high unemployment rates, the availability of guns, lack of education and inequality in the black community are examples of the aforementioned factors. [27] It has been argued by many scholars that the overall violence in American society and the poverty in the black community are contributing factors to the high homicide rate of young black males. The lack of economic opportunities for young black males has been the source of much frustration. The high homicide rate for young black males has contributed to low life expectancy for all black males in comparison to white males. Life expectancy for black males is 64.8 years, while white males can expect to live 73.6 years. [28]

HIGH UNEMPLOYMENT RATE

The unemployment rate for young black males is more than twice that of young white males. According to the latest information from the Bureau of Labor Statistics unemployment for black males ages 18 to 19 for the first quarter of the calendar year 2002 was 31.6 percent compared to 15.1 percent for white males. [29] In addition, the unemployment rate for black males ages 20 to 24 was 22.4 percent compared to 10.6 percent for white males the same age. [30]

The problems of young black males are many. Crime, violence, media images, suicide, homicide, unemployment and the lack of positive male role models are some of the issues that they face. All of these factors affect their educational pursuits and eventually their success.

STRENGTHS, WEAKNESSES, AND LIMITATIONS IN LITERATURE

SPIRITUAL

There was a dearth of literature on young black males and their spirituality. Although Toler did evaluate the men's ministry at a Baltimore church, the research focus was on the church and its pastor and not on the men of the church (although he did highlight a few examples of how the lives of the men at the church were changed). Even though the study showed an increase in the number of men who attended the church, we do not know the specific details of the before and after effects of the ministry of the church among the men at large. Walter McCray's work on the subject was more holistic in that it approached the subject from different perspectives (as explained in detail in the Proposed Theory and Rationale section of this chapter): social, psychological, spiritual, emotional, vocational, etc. However, McCray's work was heavy on theory. He did get some in depth feedback from several people, whom he included in the work, but their responses were only examples. On a larger scale, we do not know how many people were affected by his ideas and research. More research needs to be conducted using his developmental principles. Nix's work focused more on Christian psychological principles than on how the research and principles affected a group of people who had been studied.

PSYCHOLOGICAL

Several authors, who did work on psychological studies, contributed the success of young black males to church involvement or spiritual awareness. Some even emphasized the importance and the necessity to recognize the spiritual aspects of life in order to thrive in America; more research needs to be done in this area. Although it is assumed that the more a young black male is involved in spiritual activity the more success he should have, this theory has not been researched adequately and it could be argued that successful young black males are no more spiritual than average young black males.

EMOTIONAL

Several authors, such as Wade and King, gave inferences to the emotional response of young black males in different circumstances, but no study has been done that specifically dealt with this topic. King discussed violence as an emotional response of young black males to their circumstances, but he gave more of a historical overview as to how violence has affected them. It was alluded to in one study that the lack of a nurturing father—son relationship was the cause of violence among young black males.

Research on emotional disorders and young black males was lacking as well. Some information on how therapists treat young black males was discovered, but this does not answer the question of what led to the emotional problem in the first place? One study conducted by the Center for Disease Control and Prevention highlighted the rise in the suicide rate of young black males, but it did not give any definitive causes as to why the increase. The emotional health of young black males is in turmoil. Everyday young black males are responding to their crisis in negative, "pathological" ways.

The overwhelming majority of the literature that exists on young black males explores how they think and act. This literature gives great insight into the values of young black males. A better understanding is gained of the views this population has of masculinity, their relationship with their fathers, the need for role models, why they choose not to attend college, some things that distinguish average young black males from successful young black males, etc. The research in the psychology of young black males is more thorough and extensive.

CONCEPTUAL FRAMEWORK

In his book, *Black Young Adults: How to Reach Them, What to Teach Them* McCray writes about the different signs of maturity. These signs include economic independence, psychological well-being, social adjustment, accountability, emotional growth, spiritual maturity and more.[31]

HOLISTIC APPROACH TO YOUNG ADULT LIFE

Economic independence is achieved when young adults have taken the responsibility for their own economic survival through gainful employment. Psychological well-being occurs when young adults have accepted the decisions they have made concerning who they are. They are content or moving toward contentment in their lives. Socially, there is a change in their associations. As they take on the responsibility of adulthood, adults stop treating them as children. During this time, young adults usually make many mistakes, but their responses are usually different from when they were children. As young adults, they are being held responsible by society for the decisions that they make. They have attained certain rights and privileges that come with age, but they are also accountable for making sure that they take on the responsibilities that come with these rights. Emotionally, young adults encounter the unaddressed issues in their lives or in their family's lives on a more personal level. They must also deal with the consequences of their choices, whether good or bad, which can create emotional strain. How they handle emotional problems shows their maturity. Spiritually, many of the ideas and thoughts they formulated as a children are now being challenged, which may cause a reformulation or an abandonment of those ideas altogether. The process that many young adults go through should result in a more spiritually mature person.

Despite their circumstances, if young black males master the emotional, psychological and spiritual aspects of life, they will greatly increase their chances of personal success. This researcher believes that if one develops a strong sense of self one should be able to handle any problem that comes his way. Moreover, those problems that one cannot handle must be dealt within the spiritual dimension.

PRINCIPLES OF MANHOOD

In his book, *Becoming Effective Fathers and Mentors,* Sheldon Nix emphasizes the recovery, rebuilding and reconnecting process in order for black males to succeed in American society.[32] Using Systems Theory, Nix looks at politics, economics, relationships and education, to show how domination affects them. One of the steps in the recovery process is restoring purpose. It has been repeatedly proven that purpose—driven people accomplish many of their goals. This researcher believes Nix argues this point because many young black males do not know what their purpose is due to institutional racism in the workplace, academic tracking in schools and public policy that is designed to keep the poor on the bottom of the social ladder. This has caused many young black males not to pursue success.

PERSONAL DEVELOPMENT

Other points Nix discusses in this study include having a sense of self, a sense of authority or control and a sense of competence or mastery.[33] Developing a cohesive sense of self is imperative to success. Those who do have a strong sense of self can successfully go through the hard times of life with fewer battle scars than those who do not, while those who do not have a strong sense of self are usually devastated by hard times. Successful young black males have a sense of authority or control over their lives. They have the power to make their own decisions even when their options are limited. They have a goal or a plan to accomplish and they will not be deterred from their path, even by their own mistakes. When circumstances are beyond their control, they still maintain power over their reaction or response. Successful, young, black males have a sense of competence or mastery. They have developed certain skills that have allowed them to succeed in certain areas of life. Whether these skills are technical, athletic, artistic, or academic, young black males who have developed a sense of competence are more likely to succeed than those who have not mastered a particular skill. Young black males in America usually have to be achievers in order not to be stereotyped as thugs and hoodlums.

METHODOLOGY

SAMPLE

An exploratory study is being employed to get a better understanding of the values of successful, young black males in college. Behaviors, values and beliefs can be thoroughly discussed where other research methods may lead only to conclusions and assumptions. A survey was given to sixty-two young black male Clark Atlanta University students. Twelve individuals were selected from the sample to participate in—depth interviews. They were recruited to participate in this study through personal invitation based upon established rapport.

The young men all live in one of the residence halls on campus. They come from all across the country, with nearly one-quarter of them from Georgia and they range in age from eighteen to twenty-three years. They are involved in athletics, the band, the Honors Program, or other activities. Some of them have part—time jobs, some live with both parents when they are not in school and some have been in legal trouble in the past. Most of them are freshmen, while the majority of the upperclassmen are transfer students. All of them are single; some with children, but most do not have any children. Of the eighty young men who entered the residence hall, in which the study was conducted and were financially enrolled for the Fall 2001 semester, seventy-five returned and were financially enrolled for the Spring 2002 semester. Seventy-five were solicited for the purpose of this study, fifty responded. An additional twelve students who lived in the summer school residence hall also completed the survey.

INSTRUMENT

The questionnaire developed for this research was based on the Generalized Expectancy for Success Scale developed by the American Psychological Association. The questionnaire was restructured to fit the young black male population, yet the questions are broad enough to address the perception of success of black males in general. Overall, the survey includes twenty questions that were related to the students' perception of their present success. Seven questions each were asked concerning their emotional (1–7) and psychological values (8–14), while six questions were used to ascertain their spiritual values (15–20). Students had their choice of five responses ranging from strongly agree to strongly disagree. Some basic demographic information was taken from the students that included: age, hometown, classification (year in school) and race (see Appendix A).

PROCEDURE

Purposive sampling was the procedure used to conduct the research on the factors that contribute to the values of successful young black males. This is where the researcher targets a group of people specially selected for a unique purpose. The researcher never knows if the sample is representative of the population, but it is exploratory research. Individual structured interviews were conducted. The interviews lasted approximately thirty to forty-five minutes. Participants were asked a variety of questions that covered the emotional, psychological and spiritual aspects of life. All of the participants were asked the same questions. Some of the questions they were asked concerned their childhood and family life, racial identity, relationship with their friends, church involvement, the role of spirituality in their lives and how they feel as young black men in America.

The information provided by the interviewees was in some instances different from those who only responded to the questionnaire. One example of this would be their understanding of what is expected of them as men (question #8). While nearly half of them (49.2%) strongly agreed that their present success is due to their understanding of what is expected of them as men, upon further discussion many of them had questions about those expectations, thus giving the impression that they were not sure of the expectations of manhood. Based on general observation, there was no real distinction between the factors of present success (psychological, spiritual and emotional) and those from different geographical regions of the United States. An example of this would be the students from the east and the west were just as likely to attribute their present success to their spiritual beliefs as those from the south. The interviewees had a high correlation between their understanding of what it is to be an African American (question #9) and success. All of them responded affirmatively to the question, some of them are not as race—conscious as others; however, based upon their responses, none of them are in denial of their race. All of those who were interviewed agreed that what they learned as children helped to shape their spiritual beliefs and values and that it is directly correlated to their present success.

THEORY ASSUMPTIONS

The assumptions posed in this study include the following: young black males are successful because they possess values such as a sense of purpose, a sense of self, a sense of control over their lives and a sense of competence. These characteristics are manifested through hard work on the job, good grades in the classroom, a well-rounded social life and the choices that they make concerning life. Another assumption, based upon this researcher's experience in dealing with young black males, is that they do not deal adequately with the emotional, psychological and spiritual aspects of life. This could explain why there is so much research on the pathological behavior of young black males in America. This is not to say that the research is biased, because these problems do exist among young black males. However, because of their position in society, their problems are amplified. What separates successful young black males from average young black males is the degree to which their emotional, psychological and spiritual needs are addressed and met.

DEMOGRAPHIC INFORMATION

The results of the research show that the young black males who were surveyed have high levels of emotional, psychological and spiritual development. The research subjects not only think very highly of themselves, but their outlook on the future is optimistic. Before exploring the results of the research that was conducted, some basic demographic information is given. Eighty-five percent (85%) of the respondents are between the ages of eighteen and twenty (see Table 1), with the overwhelming majority being freshmen (66%); one graduate student did respond to the survey.

Table 2.1 Age of Participants

	Age	Frequency	Percent	Valid Percent	Cumulative Percent
Valid	18.00	14	22.6	23.0	23.0
	19.00	26	41.9	42.6	65.6
	20.00	12	19.4	19.7	85.2
	21.00	4	6.5	6.6	91.8
	22.00	3	4.8	4.9	96.7
	23.00	1	1.6	1.6	98.4
	24.00	1	1.6	1.6	100.0
	Total	61	98.4	100.0	
Missing	System	1	1.6		
Total		62	100.0		

All of the respondents are African-American, with the exception of one African student (see Table 2). Half of the respondents are from the South, while twenty percent (20%) are from the North. Major cities were well represented in the survey. Eight students were from Chicago, five from the New York City/Newark, New Jersey area, five from New Orleans, five are from Atlanta, and four are from an Atlanta suburb. Sixteen students are from Georgia, eight from Illinois, and five each from California, Florida, and Louisiana.

Table 2.2 Race of Participants

	Race	Frequency	Percent	Valid Percent	Cumulative Percent
Valid	African American	59	95.2	98.3	98.3
	African	1	1.6	1.7	100.0
	Total	60	96.8	100.0	
Missing	System	2	3.2		
Total		62	100.0		

The only question (#14) in which more than half of the students did not agree or strongly agree on was concerning the psychological adjustments that they have made because of racism. Many of them thought that racism was not a factor in their development at all, while nearly a quarter of the students were undecided on the effects that racism has played in their lives. Most of them felt that they could accomplish any goal that they wanted to. A significant number of respondents had mixed views on the role of church involvement in their spiritual development (question #20). A little less than half disagreed, strongly disagreed, or were undecided on whether or not church involvement contributed to their present success. These were the only two questions on the survey in which the answers of the respondents showed mixed results. At least two thirds of the respondents agreed or strongly agreed with all the rest of the questions.

ENDNOTES:

1) "News and Views: Why the Large and Growing Gender Gap in African-American Higher Education," *Journal of Blacks in Higher Education* (Spring 1998): 34.

2) Ibid.

3) Ronald Roach, "Where are the Black men on campus?" *Black Issues in Higher Education* 18, no. 6 (May 2001): 18-21.

4) *Historically Black Colleges and Universities* (New Orleans/Brunswick, ME: Wintergreen/Orchard Press, 1995), 39.

5) Clark Atlanta University Profile, Enrollment (Fall 2002). http://www.cau.edu.

6) Anthony E. O. King, "Understanding Violence among Young African-American Males: An Afrocentric Perspective," *Journal of Black Studies* 28, no. 1 (1997): 79-96.

7) Ronald Roach, "Where are the Black men on campus?" *Black Issues in Higher Education* 18, no. 6 (May 2001): 18-21.

8) "News and Views: Why the Large and Growing Gender Gap in African-American Higher Education," *Journal of Blacks in Higher Education* (Spring 1998): 34.

9) Robert Hill, *Strengths of African-American Families: Twenty – Five Years Later* (Lanham, MD: University Press of America, 1999), 85.

10) Ibid., 123.

11) Kevin B. Simms, Donice M. Knight, Jr., Katherine L. Dawes, "Institutional Factors that Influence the Academic Success of African-American Men," *Journal of Men's Studies* 1 (February 1993): 253.

12) Ronald Roach, "Where are the Black men on campus?" *Blacks Issues in Higher Education* 18, no. 6 (May 2001): 18-21.

13) Ibid.

14) H. Elaine Rodney and Robert Mupier, "Behavioral Differences between African-American Adolescents with Biological Fathers and Those without Biological Fathers in the Home," Journal *of Black Studies* 30 (September 1999): 45-61.

15) Jay C. Wade, "African-American fathers and sons: Social, Historical, and Psychological Considerations," Families *in Society* 75 (November 1994): 561.

16) Ibid.

17)   Shannette M. Harris, "Psychosocial Development and Black Male Masculinity: Implications for Counseling Economically Disadvantaged African-American Male Adolescents," *Journal of Counseling and Development* 73 (January 1995): 279.

18)   Ibid.

19)   Christine J. Yeh, "Invisibility and Self-Construal in African-American Men: Implications for Training and Practice," *Counseling Psychologist* 27 (November 1999): 810-819.

20)   W.E.B. DuBois, *The Souls of Black Folk* (Chicago: A.C. McClurg & Co., 1903), 2.

21)   Gail Elizabeth Wyatt, "Beyond Invisibility of African-American Males: The Effects on Women and Families," *Counseling Psychologist* 27 (November 1999): 802-809.

22)   Christine J. Yeh, "Invisibility and Self-Construal in African-American Men: Implications for Training and Practice," *Counseling Psychologist* 27 (November 1999): 810-819.

23)   Suicide Among Black Youths -- United States, 1980-1995, Morbidity and Mortality Weekly Report, March 20, 1998 / 47(10);193-106, Center for Disease Control and Prevention, http://www.cdc.gov/mmwr/preview/mmwrhtml/00051591.htm.

24)   Jewelle T. Gibbs, "African-American Suicide: A Cultural Paradox," *Suicide & Life - Threatening Behavior* 27 (Spring 1997) 68.

25)   *Homicide trends in the U.S.:* Age, Gender, and Race Trends (Dramatic Increases in both Homicide Victimization and Offending Rates were Experienced by Young Males, Particularly Young Black Males, in the late 1980's and early 1990's) FBI, Supplementary Homicide Reports, 1976-99, Bureau of Justice Statistics www.ojp.usdoj.gov/bjs/.

26)   Julie A Phillips, "Variation in African-American homicide rates" *Criminology* (November 1997): 527-559.

27)   Ibid.

28)   Joseph F. Aponte and Ronald T. Crouch, *Psychological Intervention and Cultural Diversity,* ed. Joseph F. Aponte and Julian Wohl (Massachusetts: Allyn and Bacon, 2000), 9.

29)   Bureau of Labor Statistics Labor Force Statistics from the Current Population Survey: Household Data Not Seasonally Adjusted Quarterly Averages. Unemployment rates by age, sex, race, and Hispanic origin. http://www.bls.gov/NLS.

30)   Ibid.

31)   Walter A. McCray, *Black Young Adults: How to Reach Them, What to Teach Them* (Chicago: Black Light Fellowship, 1992), 8-18.

32)   Sheldon Nix, *Becoming Effective Fathers and Mentors* (Woodbury, NJ: Renaissance Productions, 1996), 8.

33)   Ibid.

CHAPTER THREE
EMOTIONAL VALUES AND YOUNG BLACK MALES

LITERATURE REVIEW

There is a dearth of information on the emotional state of young black males. Much of the negative, "pathological" behavior of young black males is nothing more than an emotional response to their circumstances and environment.

RELATIONSHIP WITH THE FATHER

The father wound that exists in many young black males is deep and it is the source of much pain in their lives. Rodney and Mupier studied adolescent black males who lived with their fathers and those who did not live with their fathers. They found that "the quality of family relationships, including factors such as adequate nurturing, love and support rather than the composition of the family, influences the level of a child's self-esteem and self-concept."[1] "Furthermore, they . . . hypothesized that those youth who live in the home where the biological fathers are present will show fewer problem behaviors than do those whose biological fathers do not live in the home."[2] Their research falls in line with previous research that those who grew up with their father in the home were less likely to get into trouble in school and with the legal system. David B. Lynn's research reveals that the absence of a father through separation or divorce may lead to drug addiction, alcoholism and suicide attempts.[3] He goes on further to state, "Father—absent boys consistently performed below (scholastically) father—present boys"[4]

VIOLENCE

Violence has become a common emotional response of young black males to the way that society treats them. Many young black males have grown up in environments where they see that older black males are often unemployed for a certain period in their lives. Some common responses to unemployment are alcoholism, domestic violence and drug activity; take an emotional toll on their children. The self-destructive behavior of black males leaves few of them capable to teach young black males how to survive. Anthony E. O. King observes that "striving to mature under these social conditions often leads to unimaginable levels of confusion, personal frustration and emotional pain . . . the emotional upheaval that they endure all too often leads to an obvious sense of personal devaluation, degradation and disrespect for their lives and the lives of their peers."[5] Young black males have internalized socially acceptable media images of violence as a means of dealing with their frustrations. He further cites "the antisocial and violent behavior that characterizes the lives of hundreds of thousands of African-American male adolescents and young adults is a symptom of the extent to which they have become emotionally and socially disconnected from themselves, their cultural and historical heritage and their communities."[6] The lack of information on the emotional aspect of life does not permit me to draw an adequate conclusion on this matter. Conversely, the relationship with the father has a huge emotional toll on young black males and their success. Environmental factors, such as crime and violence, also have a great emotional influence on their success.

EMOTIONS AND YOUNG BLACK MALES

Seven questions (#1–7) on the survey focused on emotional values and the present success of young black males. The questions dealt with the respondents relationship with their father or other positive male role models, relationship with their family, relationship with their friends, their acceptance of responsibility, their attempt to resolve the emotional issues that they struggle with, their ability to handle their feelings and their maturity based upon the decisions that they make. These questions related to key areas of the emotional development of successful young black males. Primarily the questions initiated discussion about how they feel about the people in their lives contributing to their success and how they feel about their own personal decisions in relationship to their present success. As it was stated earlier in this work, young black males do not adequately cope with their emotional issues; this is probably one reason there are so few successful, young, black males.

RELATIONSHIP WITH FATHER

The relationship with the father is a source of great strain for many young black males. Unemployment, alcoholism and abuse are some of the reasons why there is emotional distance between black fathers and sons. Fathers feel most comfortable in their role when they can financially provide for their families. If a father is unemployed, he may withdraw from the family emotionally, or if he is wrapped up in his work in an effort to provide for his family, he may neglect the emotional support that fathers can give their children. As there has been a dramatic rise in the number of single female—headed households, a positive male role model such as an athletic coach, teacher, or youth leader can fill the emotional void that an absent father has left. Among the respondents, almost three-quarters (73.8%) feel that their present success is due to their father or a positive male role model (see Table 3.1).

Table 3.1 Emotional—Relationship with Father

		Frequency	Percent	Valid Per-cent	Cumulative Percent
Valid	Strongly disagree	5	8.1	8.2	8.2
	Disagree	6	9.7	9.8	18.0
	Undecided	5	8.1	8.2	26.2
	Agree	22	35.5	36.1	62.3
	Strongly agree	23	37.1	37.7	100.0
	Total	61	98.4	100.0	
Missing	System	1	1.6		
Total		62	100.0		

The responses from the interviews are varied. The student from Florida said that his father was not a "good example of a father," and that "his father motivated him through negative comments." The California student gave a similar response concerning his relationship with his father. The Florida student felt like he could not talk to his father, who has a very successful career. "My father doesn't know how to deal with stress," and he reiterates the fact that he "pay[s] the bills" for his children. Although the student has tried to be open with his father, his father is "unemotional." Meanwhile, a student from Kansas said that his, "Father has always been there for him, supported his right actions and corrected his wrong actions, explained life in general and helped him to take on responsibilities." In addition, his father gave him a lot of useful information, yet he let him learn things the hard way.

The student from Louisiana said that he and his father have had some hard times (his parents are divorced), but he has surrounded himself with men who had influence in the community. His athletic coaches helped to build the principles of manhood into him and his stepfather has been an influence in his life. The Maryland student said, "My father left my freshmen year in high school; my best friend's father played a role in my development, served as a father figure to me in high school." While a Georgia student said, "I don't live with my father; my father still gives me advice."

Like the student from Louisiana, most of the young black men who were interviewed had struggles with their fathers growing up. Several of them said that their fathers were either abusive, had children by other women that the family did not know about that was later revealed, or the fathers themselves had bad relationships with their fathers—thus impinging on their ability to be an adequate father to the young black males. Some of these relationships did get better over time, but not all. There are some deep "father wounds" that exist with several of the young men who were interviewed. The resiliency of the students from Florida and California is evident in their attempt to achieve their goals in spite of not crediting their fathers or a particular male role model as to their present success. They exhibit a persistence to achieve something positive for themselves.

RELATIONSHIP WITH FAMILY

The black family in America has been the victim of many social, political and economic attacks. Yet, until recently, it sustained itself through most of these attacks. The extended family has traditionally been the norm for African Americans. How has the black family been able to support these young men? In spite of the relationship with their fathers, the support that comes from other family members has helped to buffer these young men from failure. More than eighty-eight percent of the students, (88.7%), agreed or strongly agreed that their family played a significant role in their present success (see Table 3.2).

Table 3.2 Emotional—Relationship with Family

		Frequency	Percent	Valid Per-cent	Cumulative Percent
Valid	Strongly disagree	2	3.2	3.2	3.2
	Undecided	5	8.1	8.1	11.3
	Agree	21	33.9	33.9	45.2
	Strongly agree	34	54.8	54.8	100.0
Total		62	100.0	100.0	

One of the students from California said, "His sisters and his mom have pushed him" to achieve. The Florida student said that his "mother is supportive," and that he has a close relationship with his brothers. A student from Virginia said, "All of his success is due to family." They have been there for him and he is able to talk to them. The student from Louisiana stated that his family "never let me go off into things that were harmful, they looked out for my best interest." The student from Georgia echoed the same sentiments about his family. Another California student expressed, "My father and my brother inspire me to do what I am doing, I don't want my family see me fail." A student from Colorado articulated that his "family relationships are strong, except for money [issues]." A student from Texas, who currently has a 4.0 GPA, said that he is not close to his family. "My mother was in and out of his life," he says and he does not get along with his brother.

This student's response falls in line with the research of this study, not all of the students have strong family ties. However, most of the students gave the impression that without familial support they would not be able to pursue their goals. Brothers and sisters, most often mentioned, made sure that these young men had the adequate support that they needed and that they stayed out of legal trouble as much as possible. Although only a few students referenced their mothers as a source of their present success, none of the students had anything negative to say about their mothers.

Very little was specifically said about the influence of the extended family. The student from Kansas has great communication with his paternal grandfather and he has learned a lot about business from him (his grandfather owns the family business). "My family (on his paternal grandfather's side) takes care of each other." He also has a close relationship with his maternal grandparents. His maternal grandmother helped to raise him when he was young. In addition, he believes "my extended family has taught me a lot," they often pray together at family reunions. The Florida student said that although he knows his maternal aunts and uncles, "I have no relationship with my extended family."

RELATIONSHIP WITH FRIENDS

Friends come and go throughout a normal lifespan. What impact do these friends make? Have they built the students up, or torn them down? The students were much less likely to say that their present success is due to friendships that they have formed over the years. In fact, more than thirty-five percent (35.5%) disagreed, strongly disagreed, or were undecided about the contribution their friends have had on their present success.

Table 3.3 Emotional—Relationship with Friends

		Frequency	Percent	Valid Percent	Cumulative Percent
Valid	Strongly disagree	4	6.5	6.5	6.5
	Disagree	5	8.1	8.1	14.5
	Undecided	13	21.0	21.0	35.5
	Agree	29	46.8	46.8	82.3
	Strongly agree	11	17.7	17.7	100.0
Total		62	100.0	100.0	

The majority of the students have a close circle of friends that they spoke of highly. The student from Maryland credits his friends for giving him "right insight," and helping him with many decisions. The Georgia student has friends who "are on the same level as I am, they are going through the same things that I am and they have the same ambitions." The student from Texas believes he would not be who he is today without his friends. "My friends push me to achieve and give him the support that I need." The Virginia student stated his "friends bring out his competitive drive." The Louisiana student feels that he and his friends "pushed each other to be the best." They studied together because they knew they were going to go to college and be successful. They did not want to disappoint themselves and their families. One of the California students also did not want his friends to see him fail.

Several of the students had very different views of the correlation between friendship and their present success. The student from Colorado had mixed feelings about friendships. "Deception and friendship go hand in hand," he stated.

Many people have hurt him. He did acknowledge that he had some friends who "helped me through some dark times and taught me patience." As a result, he is willing to give people a chance to prove themselves. The other California student "understands the consequences of decisions that groups can make," and he does not "go with the group." The Kansas student believed that he "can't really call anyone a true friend," he has associates. He pretty much stays to himself. His previous friends "were into the wrong things." However, after some thought, he did recall one really good friend that he can talk to about anything. The Florida student also does not have too many friends. He feels that "some friends are only there for entertainment." He does place a high value "on those who are there with me through the tough times."

ACCEPTANCE OF RESPONSIBILITY

The ability to accept responsibility moves one from immaturity to maturity. It forces one to either stand up, or sit down. Responsibility carries with it a weight, or an obligation. One loses something when he accepts responsibility; usually it is freedom. How then could this loss contribute to success? Most of the respondents (86.9%) agreed or strongly agreed that they accept responsibility and that was a reason why they are presently successful.

Table 3.4 Emotional—Acceptance of Responsibility

		Frequency	Percent	Valid Percent	Cumulative Percent
Valid	Strongly disagree	1	1.6	1.6	1.6
	Disagree	2	3.2	3.3	4.9
	Undecided	5	8.1	8.2	13.1
	Agree	25	40.3	41.0	54.1
	Strongly agree	28	45.2	45.9	100.0
	Total	61	98.4	100.0	
Missing	System	1	1.6		
Total		62	100.0		

The student from Georgia believes, "If you are willing to accept responsibility, you're willing to face life, handle whatever outcome." The student from Colorado knows he is responsible for his actions. "If I didn't have responsibility I would be nothing," he declares. Several other students affirm that they are accountable for their decisions. "No one else is going to accept responsibility for me," says the student from Texas. One of the California students said, "Whatever I do I am responsible for it." The student from Florida took the spiritual route in reference to responsibility, "God will judge you alone," he states. The Virginia student believes a person "can't go forward without accepting responsibility." The student from Louisiana said that he used to make excuses for things, but now he realizes that not accepting responsibility is a reflection on him. While the other student from California is still trying to understand all the responsibility he has. "I have to work to pay my bills, but I know I'm not grown yet." Having known most of the young men, who were interviewed, as researcher and resident assistant in a dormitory, they believe that they are grown men—they say it all the time. In addition, most of them are willing to accept responsibility, even if they get into trouble, most of the time.

RESOLVING ISSUES

The resolution of personal issues is of vital importance to the success of young black men. Many black males have gone before them and have had professional success, only to be brought down by an issue in their personal life that they had been struggling with for years, but was never resolved. Whether it is R. Kelly, Jesse Jackson, Michael Irving, Henry Lyons, or Allen Iverson, many successful black men, from all lifestyles, have been humiliated because of a lack character. This is part of the reason for the mistrust between the current generation and their father's generation; there are not enough role models with personal integrity. Many have adopted the behaviors of their elders as a coping mechanism with life. They see their personal and private lives as being two separate entities. "As long as you are able to do your job effectively, it should not matter what you do off the clock," they say. This philosophy is often used as a loophole to avoid building character and dealing with the issues that could "come back to haunt them later in life."

Everyone has issues; some people just do not realize it. To recognize that one has a personal issue can be devastating to some. One realizes that he is not who he thought he was. Attempting to bring resolution to a personal issue can consume a lot of time and it can be agonizing. Almost three-quarters (73.8%) of the respondents believe that their present success is due to their attempt to resolve personal issues.

Table 3.5 Emotional—Resolving Issues

		Frequency	Percent	Valid Percent	Cumulative Percent
Valid	Strongly disagree	2	3.2	3.3	3.3
	Disagree	2	3.2	3.3	6.6
	Undecided	12	19.4	19.7	26.2
	Agree	17	27.4	27.9	54.1
	Strongly agree	28	45.2	45.9	100.0
	Total	61	98.4	100.0	
Missing	System	1	1.6		
Total		62	100.0		

The student from Virginia "needs to find out the details in everything" in order to resolve issues. He has to understand the problem before he can solve it. "Most problems are a misunderstanding or a lack of knowledge," he feels. In addition, he views any experience as a learning experience. "I can feel when hard times come," the Colorado student states, realizing that obstacles are apart of life that you must encounter. One of the California students believes that if he does not correct his mistakes he "will never be successful." The Maryland student emphasizes, "You got to try, dust yourself off and try again." The student from Georgia understands that he is strong in some areas and weak in others. "I am willing to make the necessary changes to be a better person." The other California student says, "I used to have a real short temper and wouldn't listen to reason." Now he is able to control his temper and accept the truth without "getting hotheaded." Now he sees other people act as he used to act and he realizes that he has matured. "I am able to control my temper now."

The resolution of personal issues is a necessary part of character building and if young black males are going to be successful in this country, they are going to need character. Additionally, they are going to have to control their feelings.

HANDLE FEELINGS

Feelings can be fickle. An individual may not understand why he is feeling what he is feeling; all he knows is that he is feeling it. How does an individual handle the way he responds to these circumstance, situations, and/or things? Is he passive, aggressive, or even-tempered? How can one's response to his feelings bring him success? According to the survey, more than seventy-eight percent (78.7%) agreed or strongly agreed that their present success was due to their ability to handle their feelings effectively (see Table 3.6). This traditionally has been a weak area for men, so it was surprising to see what these young black men think of their ability to control their emotions.

Table 3.6 Emotional—Handle Feelings

		Frequency	Percent	Valid Percent	Cumulative Percent
Valid	Strongly disagree	3	4.8	4.9	4.9
	Disagree	1	1.6	1.6	6.6
	Undecided	9	14.5	14.8	21.3
	Agree	28	45.2	45.9	67.2
	Strongly agree	20	32.3	32.8	100.0
	Total	61	98.4	100.0	
Missing	System	1	1.6		
Total		62	100.0		

An anonymous student, that was one of the twelve original students that were interviewed, confessed that he might potentially be a father. When asked further about the becoming a father, he said, "I will take care of my responsibilities and I have no plans of dropping out of college." He also implied that he tries to remain calm in different circumstances, "you will get more done by staying calm," he said. The student from Colorado had feelings that ran the emotional gamut, from crying to sheer rage. "Crying is a natural response for me." He has taken up the art of boxing and has begun meditation in an attempt to control the rage inside of him. He does not get as angry as quickly anymore. One of the students from California does not show his feelings most of the time. "In the corporate office you can't say whatever; you have to think before you speak." The student from Maryland believes "you got to have self-control because people will push you buttons." You cannot react in anger all of the time because "that's not how society operates." The Virginia student has grown to understand how to deal with his feelings at the right time. "You have to stay level—headed," he states, "and think through situations." The student from Louisiana affirmed that he knows how to handle his feelings in different situations, "but if I get frustrated I'm going to show my frustration," he blurts.

MATURE DECISIONS

Decisions are a part of life. A positive decision will make you happy; a negative decision can cost you time and money. The kind of decisions that one makes shows to others their mindset. Do I do what is right, or do I take the least painful way out of a situation? If I make a mistake do I take responsibility for it, or do I blame someone else? The last question on the survey that attempted to explore the emotional values of successful young black males concerned their ability to make mature decisions. Nearly ninety percent (88.7%) agreed or strongly agreed that they have made mature decisions that have led to their present success.

Table 3.7 Emotional—Mature Decisions

		Frequency	Percent	Valid Percent	Cumulative Percent
Valid	Strongly disagree	3	4.8	4.9	4.9
	Disagree	1	1.6	1.6	6.6
	Undecided	3	4.8	4.9	11.5
	Agree	25	40.3	41.0	52.5
	Strongly agree	29	46.8	47.5	100.0
	Total	61	98.4	100.0	
Missing	System	1	1.6		
Total		62	100.0		

The student from Colorado articulated that he is growing in maturity. "I recognize that the R.O.T.C. was a bad decision for me and Adams State University was not for me. The student from Virginia comments, "That smoking in the dormitory room was a poor decision." It helped him to focus on what is important for him, which is college. The student from Georgia states, "That in certain cases bad decisions can help you learn." Mistakes help you grow, he expressed. The student from Louisiana looks at the consequences of a decision beforehand. "Like sex, I think before I act."

EMOTIONAL VALUES ASSESSMENT

Overall, the students showed high levels of emotional maturity in their personal decisions and they were able to acknowledge the people who helped them to be successful. The relationship between the students and their fathers was less than harmonious, but some of the students are trying to work through that relationship. Very few of the interviewees had positive things to say about their fathers. However, males in the extended family or positive male role models have filled in the gaps that biological fathers left unfulfilled. Family was absolutely crucial to the success of young black males; even more so than the relationship with the father or other positive male role model, according to the survey. Without the strong family, as described by Hill, it appears that many of these young black males may not be pursuing their goal of graduating from college. The research indicates that friendships were not as important to their success as family. The ability to conduct themselves in a mature manner was very important to the students and their success. While they are still trying to work out personal issues in their lives, they showed positive responses to reacting to them. In other words, they are trying to work out what is being experienced emotionally, by not running away from responsibility, realizing that it is a necessary part of character development. Many of them indicated that they are mature beyond their years, while one may not have gotten that impression from their actions, they did give the impression that they knew what they believed about themselves and their present success.

CONCLUSION

The results of the research are in agreement with current research on young black males and their relationship with their families. Maton, Hrabowski, and Grief point out that parental involvement is related to academic success.[7] The young black males who were interviewed believed that familial support helped them achieve their goal of going to college. The constant encouragement of family members, the boundaries that they set for the students and the emotional support that was given during the times of trials helped to contribute to the present success of the young black males surveyed. The results on father—son relationships were more complex than the previous research on this subject. Much of the previous research focused on the father—son relationship, to the exclusion of other positive male role models. Many of these young men did not grow up with their fathers, but they did have positive male influences in their lives. For many of the students, stepfathers filled the void that was left when their father left their families for various reasons. Other students, those without a stepfather, did remain in contact with their fathers even though there was geographic distant between them. Still others had positive male role models who influenced them. Communication with fathers or other positive male role models was vital to the success of these young black males. Most of the students felt that they had an older male in their lives to whom they could they could talk. In addition, for some, as Rodney and Mupier observe, the extended family played an important role in the lives of young black males.[8] Some of the students did have extended family members who played a role in their development. The relationship between successful young black males and their friends needs further exploration. In addition, how young black males feel about responsibility, their own emotional issues and feelings and the decisions they have to make as they mature needs more in depth study. The generality of the questions on responsibility, emotional issues, personal feelings and mature decisions did not uncover any conclusive research as to how these factors contribute to their emotional development.

ENDNOTES:

1)   H. Elaine Rodney and Robert Mupier, "Behavioral Differences between African-American Adolescents with Biological Fathers and Those without Biological Fathers in the Home," *Journal of Black Studies* 30 (September 1999): 45-61.

2)   Ibid.

3)   David B. Lynn, *The Father: His Role in Child Development* (Monterey, CA: Brooks/Cole, 1974), 265.

4)   Ibid., 272.

5)   Anthony E. O. King, "Understanding Violence among Young African-American Males: An Afrocentric Perspective," *Journal of Black Studies* 28 (September 1997): 79-96.

6)   Ibid.

7)   Kenneth I. Maton, Freeman A. Hrabowski III, Geoffrey L. Greif, "Preparing the way: A qualitative study on high—achieving African-American males and the role of the family," Journal *of Community Psychology* 26 (August 1998): 639-668

8)   H. Elaine Rodney and Robert Mupier, "Behavioral differences between African-American adolescents with biological fathers and those without biological fathers in the home," *Journal of Black Studies* 30 (September 1999): 45-61.

CHAPTER FOUR
PSYCHOLOGICAL VALUES AND YOUNG BLACK MALES

LITERATURE REVIEW

FACTORS IN EDUCATIONAL SUCCESS

The overwhelming majority of the literature that was found discussed the psychology of young black males. According to W. F. Sedlacek "variables that are unique in contributing to minority students' success in higher education: a positive self-concept, understanding and dealing with racism, a realistic self-appraisal, the availability of a strong support person.[1] Simms, Knight, and Dawes argue that academic and personal support services (including faculty mentoring, academic adjustment, skill deficiency programs and special orientation sessions) were important and necessary to the academic success of black males. They also recommended that the educational curriculum used in teaching black males include a multicultural worldview.[2] This would include solving problems from different perspectives, which the author asserts is one of the best ways in which black males learn.

NON-ACADEMIC FACTORS

In contrast, Clyde W. Franklin and C. Andre Mizell, give some non-academic factors that influence the success of black males. These include "positive levels of self-esteem, a supportive family structure, various coping strategies, an awareness of discrimination and a degree of religiosity."[3] They emphasize a positive self-esteem and a positive self-concept because racial issues in America still prohibit black males from succeeding. They examined the above factors to see how they affect social mobility. They found that a positive self-esteem, religious beliefs and an awareness of racism are some of the factors that contribute to social mobility for black males.[4] Many whites will not allow blacks to move forward in society because they believe that blacks are the cause of their own problems. Blaming the victim, crime and the apathy of the black middle—class are often cited as the reasons why blacks do not excel in American society.

INSTITUTIONAL RACISM

Institutional racism continues to be the overarching factor that prohibits the rise of black males socially.[5] Institutional racism can be defined as the structures that are set within the different institutions (private business, legal system, local and federal government) of American society that are designed to discriminate against minorities in America. This is visible in "Corporate America", very few black males are able to break the "glass ceiling" and obtain jobs in upper—level management. Even more evident is the disproportionate number of young black males who are involved in the legal system in comparison to young white males (as previously discussed in the Background of the Problem). This affirms why many young black males are choosing professions outside of the private business field. Institutional racism is a factor in the high crime rate among young black males. Many young black males cannot get a job that pays an adequate living wage; therefore, many choose to get rich quick by becoming involved in the drug trade. As a result, many young black males are involved in the legal system. Conversely, successful blacks have created problems for blacks that have not excelled within the American system. As the black middle—class continues to grow in America, their success has not only created a gulf between the haves and have—nots in black America, but many Americans who recognize the division see poor blacks as lazy (a common stereotype for the poor). The success of some blacks has given many whites a reason to continue, "blaming the victim" for his lack of achievement.

PERSONAL AND SOCIAL FACTORS

Self-esteem has a correlated effect on success and social mobility, as stated earlier by Franklin and Mizell. According to conventional wisdom, blacks that have high self-esteem have a better chance at achieving their goals than those with low self-esteem. Blacks who have high self-esteem are aware of the racism that exists in society, are proud to be black and have developed values that have allowed them to continue to pursue their goals in life; they are more likely to be successful in America as a result. Some black men have attempted to deny their identity in order to gain acceptance in American society by trying to make their racial and ethnic identity invisible in the hope that people will accept them as individuals.[6] This coping mechanism has led to a hatred of anything that is black. Assimilation into American society usually results in self-hatred of things that are reminiscent of ethnic affiliation in order not to be objectionable to white America.[7] Social buffers, such as family and friends, help to create an environment that helps to foster mental stability in stressful situations. Franklin and Mizell believe "social buffers insulate the individual African-American male. They provide protection from the hostility and psychological undermining of mainstream society by creating networks and groups in the African-American community where humanity, care and concern can become rooted and grow."[8]

FATHER'S ROLE

Wade states, "The majority of studies on African-American fathers focus on the negative consequences of the fathers' absence from the family"[9] These consequences usually reveal themselves in psychosocial behavioral patterns such as disruptive behavior in class and poor academic performance. In traditional African society, the father played a prominent role in raising their sons. They taught their sons the skills that were necessary for their survival. The older men taught the younger men what their interpretation of a man was and this instruction was passed down through the generations. In American society, fathers are more concerned with providing for their families and the more money a father makes, the more confident he is in his role as a provider.[10] Many scholars believe that urbanization and industrialization have contributed to the break up of the black family. In addition, societal factors such as racism, lack of employment and economic opportunities have also contributed to the rift in the black family. "Historically, however, social conditions have made it extremely difficult for African-American men to achieve economic self-sufficiency and, therefore, to play an authoritative role within the family."[11] Black men who cannot provide for their families often see themselves as failures and they react to their failure negatively, which in turn has a huge impact on the family. According to Wade, "If African-American men cannot negotiate a life for themselves and their family within the existing social structure; they may react negatively by withdrawing from the family or abusing it, resort to a life of crime, develop outside relationships with other women, and/or resort to self-destructive acts of suicide and substance abuse."[12]

FAMILY'S ROLE

Some young black males become attached to their fathers in childhood. Black fathers serve as heroes to their sons. The child's frame of reference for identity development is the father. Young black males who grow up in homes where the father is present are more likely to succeed in life and less likely to get into legal trouble.[13] However, even homes where the father is absent, the extended family support network can prove beneficial to the success of African-American males. In many cases grandfathers, uncles and older cousins can provide the needed emotional support to produce healthy levels of self-esteem in African-American males. Deborah Brown, Hutchinson, Valutis, and White argue, "It is not the structure of the family itself that causes [negative] behaviors, but the relationships within the structure."[14] Rodney and Mupier assert, "The quality of family relationships . . . influences the level of a child's self-esteem and self-concept."[15]

Kenneth I. Maton, Hrabowski, and Greif believe that parental involvement in academics, the style of parenting, the make up of the family and community factors are linked to academic achievement among black adolescents.[16] Young black males who had parents who were involved in their child's education were more likely to achieve in school. Parents who are strict, yet supportive of their children are more likely to have high achieving black males academically. The environment that young black males grow up in has a huge impact on their success academically. The family's socio—economic status is also a factor. The higher the family income, the more likely the children will do well in school or attend college. Research shows that love and support, particularly from mothers, was a significant factor in the development of successful black males.[17] The affection that they receive at home appears to be a social buffer that has allowed them to go out and achieve their goals.

PEER'S AND TEACHER'S ROLE

One factor that has been overlooked in the academic success of African-American males is peer relations. Those who have friends who do well in school are more likely to attend college, while those who have friends who do not place value in education, did not themselves value education. Schoolteachers also have a huge influence on successful, black males. Young black males hold teachers who motivate them to achieve in high regard. On the other hand, very few young black males attend college. Research shows one of the reasons why young black males do not attend college is because of the poor treatment they received in high school from teachers, administrators and counselors.[18] Many young black males who simply refuse to attempt to go to college have internalized the constant reinforcement of the perception of being stupid. This belief system was introduced to them in primary and secondary schools and they have responded emotionally by not yielding themselves to further devaluation by others.

RESILIENCY

Wyatt writes, "Racial acceptance of Black males seemed to require that they be athletes or entertainers. Glimpses of the average African-American male (father, co—worker, and student) were rare. He had to have unusual skills or talents to be acceptable."[19] Resiliency is another factor often overlooked in successful, young, black males. Despite poverty, crime, unemployment and other negative situations, Anderson, Eaddy, and Williams note "most African-American youths grow up to be well-functioning and productive adults."[20]

EUROCENTRIC PSYCHOLOGY

Shannette M. Harris and Majors assert that white psychology has been the basis of the laws, policies, rules and regulations.[21] This psychology has had a detrimental impact on black males in the form of racism, prejudice and discrimination. The future time oriented, long-range planning, competitive, impersonal, individualistic, materialistic world of European-Americans is vastly different from the past and present time oriented, short—term planning, cooperative, emotional, community focused world of African-Americans.[22] Black males are not as likely to sacrifice, as others are in order to achieve their goals and advance in society. The focus of black psychology is on the group, which is contrary to the individualistic achievement orientation of the private business world, which may require black males to leave their family and friends and move to another city in order for them to advance in their careers.[23]

POVERTY

C. Andre Mizell found that poverty and parental educational attainment have a great influence on the self-concept of young black males. Poor families do not have the necessary resources that it takes to make sure that their children succeed, such as money or the right social network.[24] The lack of educational and economic opportunities for young black males leads to a low sense of control over their environment, which leads to negative, "pathological" behavior.

ASSIMILATION INTO AMERICAN SOCIETY

Ronald L. Taylor argued in the 1970s that the advancement of the black race during that time created developmental problems in black young adults. The growth of the black professional class, the increase in the number of blacks enrolled in colleges and universities and the recent social changes in the nation created a new dynamic that was unfamiliar to black young adults.[25] Taylor further explains that the lack of black role models in these groundbreaking arenas, coupled with the new demands and expectations that were placed on them by the new opportunities that arose created an identity crisis.[26] Black young adults had to justify race consciousness with economic and social advancement. Young adults are idealistic; they are actively looking for people to follow and believe in. Selecting a role model, as well as the development of a personal ideology, are pressing issues in young adulthood. As stated earlier, the primary role model for young black males is the father. However, as they grow older young black males begin to see flaws in their father's character, which causes them to evaluate their father's life.[27]

INFLUENCE OF PEER GROUPS

Harris points out that young black males today have redefined masculinity to emphasize sexual promiscuity and violence, in part due to the lack of black male role models.[28] The aggressive behavior of many black men stands in sharp contrast to the passive behavior of the rest of American society. Many young black males feel anger and resentment because of their environmental situations, which has been the cause of their dependence on peer groups. Peer groups offer a sense of belonging and security to further young black males. It is within this group that social interaction skills that were taught at home are further developed and they are able to form an identity, through which they resolve masculine traits.

DEVALUATION OF EDUCATION

Academic success has its limits, as many realize that the "glass—ceiling" in the work place prohibits them from attaining their goals.[29] Therefore, work experience may be sporadic and dissimilar. The fact that black males are portrayed as athletes and entertainers in American society contributes to the non-academic pursuits of young black males, as young black males see that they can make more money by becoming a professional athlete or entertainer. Intellectual aspirations are seen as being passive; standards and norms have traditionally required students to behave in a manner consistent with stereotypical feminine gender role behaviors and this does not equate with the aggressive behavior that many young black males exhibit.[30] Although it is commonly known that education is the best way for blacks to succeed in America, many young black males do not place any value in it and they end up living out some of the negative stereotypes that were mentioned previously in this work in chapter two.

In understanding the psychology of successful, young, black males we have examined the affects of academic success, social mobility, the role of the father and the family, the influence of the peer group, the lack of positive male role models and how high self-esteem and other factors contribute to the development of successful, young, black males.

PSYCHOLOGY AND YOUNG BLACK MALES

The seven questions (#8–14) on the survey dealing with the psychological factors and the present success of young black males related to the participants' understanding of what is expected of them as men, what it means to be an African-American, the sense of control they have over their lives, knowledge of their strengths and weaknesses, positive self-esteem, competence in their skills and abilities and the adjustments they have made because of racism. The first two questions deal with their understanding of what they think of themselves conceptually, who they believe they are. Do they try to categorize themselves, or do they live outside of the boundaries that society has (whether good or bad)? The last set of questions (#10–14) inquires about the knowledge they have of themselves and their abilities.

EXPECTATIONS OF MANHOOD

Manhood is an abstract concept that adult males attempt to attain. In traditional African societies the men, or elders, of the village would take the young boys away from their families for a period and train them in the ways of manhood. In today's American culture this practice is not readily done. An organized format to train young boys in the ways of manhood does not exist to the same extent as it did in traditional African societies, even though rites of passage programs for young black males are emerging throughout the country. Manhood in America is something caught rather than taught; in other words, manhood is learned by watching other men, not through personal instruction. This leaves room for individual interpretation of what manhood is. This was evident in the responses of the young men that were interviewed. While those who were surveyed answered the question affirmatively, upon more in—depth interviews most of the students only had ideals of what a man should be. Nearly a quarter (24.6%) of the respondents struggle with the concept of manhood and what is expected of them, while about half (50.8%) strongly agreed that there understanding of manhood has contributed to their present success (see Table 4.1).

Table 4.1 Psychological—Expectations of Manhood

		Frequency	Percent	Valid Per-cent	Cumulative Percent
Valid	Strongly disagree	2	3.2	3.3	3.3
	Disagree	3	4.8	4.9	8.2
	Undecided	10	16.1	16.4	24.6
	Agree	15	24.2	24.6	49.2
	Strongly agree	31	50.0	50.8	100.0
	Total	61	98.4	100.0	
Missing	System	1	1.6		
Total		62	100.0		

A student from Virginia states that he has "some understanding of what it is to be a man. College has helped me to become a better man, by making me more responsible for what I do." However, he admits, "no one is making sure that you do certain things," a sign that he wants to be held accountable for moving forward in his manhood. One of the students from California confesses, "I am still struggling with the concept of manhood. People say be a man to fit the situation they are in." The student from Louisiana feels "black men aren't fulfilling their roles" as men and he questions some of the purposes of older men. He personally believes that he should inspire those younger than he is. He also believes that "a man should serve God, build family and make the people around him better." A student from Maryland knows what is expected of him as a man, "being responsible, taking care of business, it's just whether you choose to do it or not." The parents of the Florida student expected certain things of him. They taught him to believe that "a man should be independent, mature, spiritually developed and respectful to women." The parents of the student from Georgia told him about certain characteristics that make up a man, these include: "responsibility and hard work for your family and knowing this I try to live up to it" he acknowledges. The student from Colorado believes that survival is an expectation of manhood. "Manhood is being true to yourself, realizing what you have to do in life, facing the facts." He understands that there are repercussions to his actions.

UNDERSTANDING OF BEING BLACK

A description of the descendents of the African slaves in America has changed over the centuries since they first arrived here. "Which name attributes to your understanding of your identity, 'black' or 'African-American'?" Even more important, do they identify themselves as such, that is as African American, with all of the inferences, limitations and advantages that it carries. More than a quarter (27.9%) respondents admitted that they did not understand what it is to be an African American (see Table 4.2).

Table 4.2 Psychological—Understanding of Being Black

		Frequency	Percent	Valid Percent	Cumulative Percent
Valid	Strongly disagree	1	1.6	1.6	1.6
	Disagree	3	4.8	4.9	6.6
	Undecided	13	21.0	21.3	27.9
	Agree	19	30.6	31.1	59.0
	Strongly agree	25	40.3	41.0	100.0
	Total	61	98.4	100.0	
Missing	System	1	1.6		
Total		62	100.0		

The student from Florida understands what it is to be African-American, but he exclaims, "I'm not really big on it." "It is something I have to live as, not something I think of constantly." One of the students from California, who is actually Jamaican exclaims, "Africans don't want us to be called African and Americans don't want us to be called Americans." The student from Virginia identifies that not "everything is going to come easy for you." He uses it as motivation to achieve, not as an excuse; it drives him to do better. The student from Louisiana believes that color does not matter. However, "black males should teach other black males about their life experiences" he implies. The student from Maryland knows that he is a minority. "In order to bring himself and his people up he is going to step up the game." The student from Georgia wants to prove people wrong. "A lot of white people expect blacks to act in a certain way—loud, rude and disrespectful; but blacks are superior," he states, "in that no matter what they try to do to us we continue to thrive. Blacks can do things that they don't expect us to." The student from Colorado brings some philosophical depth to the concept of being an African- American. "Black-American, African-Americans, needs to understand what it is to be African, the politics behind being African in America. As a mulatto I take pride in being African, I'm thankful also of the European [side of me]. I will keep unlocking my African roots spiritually and mentally. Being black is in the heart and mind. To be African you need to know history, origin, or you will be like a tree without any roots." He shows his pride in being African, yet he admits, "Being African-American can be very confusing to a mulatto." An example would be working with people at Paschal's Restaurant who were in the Civil Rights Movement, who still use the word 'nigga.' He does not understand why they use that word. "I try not to use the word 'nigga,'" he explains.

SENSE OF CONTROL

Powerlessness is the feeling of watching injustice happen to someone, or yourself and not having the ability to change the circumstances. At the heart of the question (#10) dealing with the sense of control the students have in their lives is do you own yourself, or does someone else own you? For students this is a hard question to agree with because most of them are not paying for their education. Despite this limitation, the question seeks to find out if they are making their own decisions concerning their life, or are there outside influences from society, their family, and/or their own fear. Almost three-quarters (74.2%) of the students thought that they have a sense of control over their lives (see Table 4.3).

Table 4.3 Psychological—Sense of Control

		Frequency	Percent	Valid Percent	Cumulative Percent
Valid	Strongly disagree	2	3.2	3.2	3.2
	Undecided	14	22.6	22.6	25.8
	Agree	23	37.1	37.1	62.9
	Strongly agree	23	37.1	37.1	100.0
Total		62	100.0	100.0	

One of the students from California says, "My dad gave me enough freedom so that I have a sense of control over my life," while the student from Florida admits that he is not fully independent because his dad pays for college. The parents of the Louisiana student also allowed him to have control over his life. However, he admits, "My trust with my mother only goes as far as I lose it; I'm not trying to lose it." The student from Maryland realizes that he does not have control over his life. "I don't have what I want. I am in control, but I'm not controlling [my life]." The student from Colorado can feel the restrictions around him. "I don't like restrictions," he asserts. "You have control but there are only certain points when you don't have control, society takes control from you." The student from Georgia believes that everybody has control over his life. However, he accepts the fact that some things you cannot control, "you just have to roll with it, you have to try and overcome it like being born in poverty." The student from Florida does not feel that he has complete control of his life. "Nevertheless, I do take risks because of the control I feel I have." He has control in academics, but he is conscious of the fact that you cannot control people in a relationship. The student from Virginia states he does have control over his life. "I feel like I can do whatever I want. My success is totally dependent on me – football, graduation." The student from Texas feels that he has limited control over his life. "I don't have control over . . . the money for school." While the other student from California believes that, someone has already mapped out his life. "If you know the beginning and the end, why go through the motions?" he asks. "It's kind of hard to believe that I don't have control over my life. Things happen for a reason," he expresses. "Different outcomes could happen based on the decisions that you make." The student from Kansas feels he is independent. "I don't like to depend on others," he states. He is open to suggestions and he is willing to learn from his mistakes, but he is his own individual. His philosophy is "do not let anything control you but yourself." Overall, the students believe that they are in control of their life and their destiny.

STRENGTHS AND WEAKNESSES

To know one's strengths and weaknesses is the first step to self-knowledge. This question asks if the students are familiar with their gifts, abilities, personality, tendencies and idiosyncrasies. Are they aware of the areas in their lives that they need to build up, things they need to stay away from, talents they need to share with others? Just about eighty percent (79%) of the students said that their present success is due to the knowledge of their strengths and weaknesses (see Table 4.4).

Table 4.4 Psychological—Strengths and Weaknesses

		Frequency	Percent	Valid Percent	Cumulative Percent
Valid	Disagree	2	3.2	3.2	3.2
	Undecided	11	17.7	17.7	21.0
	Agree	28	45.2	45.2	66.1
	Strongly agree	21	33.9	33.9	100.0
Total		62	100.0	100.0	

The student from Florida says, "He focuses on the things that he is good in and is dependent on others in his weak areas." An example would be group presentations; he allows others to do the things that he is weak in, like public speaking. The student from Virginia says, "He doesn't have a full grasp of his strengths and weaknesses." Although he knows himself pretty well, there are things that he tries to do that just do not fit him. "I am learning from life and experience." The student from Louisiana is acquainted with his strengths and weaknesses. "I'm not going to jump into a pool to save someone if I know I can't swim. I won't out think a philosopher, because it's not my field." He tries not to be overconfident with his strengths and weaknesses because he knows it will lead him to pride. The student from Maryland reveals, "I try to stay away from my weaknesses, they are my greatest enemy." "But at the same time I try to build them up." The student from Georgia explains, "When you're blind to your weaknesses it can hold you back. God gives everybody a gift. Once you realize your strengths, you can exploit them. When you know your strengths and weaknesses all you can do is try to get better." The student from Colorado says he is a perfectionist. "I don't dwell on my strengths, but my weaknesses kill me." He is shocked when someone notices his strengths. He is striving for perfection, "I want to be in tune with nutrition, I meditate, I want to understand myself."

POSITIVE SELF-ESTEEM

Positive self-esteem refers to valuing oneself for who he really is. Individuals believe that they have worth to others, God, and/or themselves. Even with flaws, these individuals are headed toward a goal and are content with where they are. These individuals are secure with themselves and they are still growing. Their beliefs and values are at the root of their positive self-esteem. Their worth is derived from what they believe in and what they believe about themselves. Attributing positive self-esteem to the present success of the students who responded to the survey was extremely high. More than ninety percent (90.3%) reported having positive self-esteem (see Table 4.5).

Table 4.5 Psychological—Self-Esteem

		Frequency	Percent	Valid Percent	Cumulative Percent
Valid	Disagree	2	3.2	3.2	3.2
	Undecided	4	6.5	6.5	9.7
	Agree	23	37.1	37.1	46.8
	Strongly agree	33	53.2	53.2	100.0
Total		62	100.0	100.0	

One of the students from California says, "I have good self-esteem, its high." He further states, "It goes along with knowing your strengths and weaknesses." The student from Louisiana feels, "I can always be better than the next person, I'm my only obstacle." The students from Georgia and Colorado are positive thinkers. The student from Virginia declares, "You can't do anything if you don't believe in yourself." The student from Maryland states, "I have no self-esteem. I probably wouldn't have done half the things I have done if I had positive self-esteem, like when I began smoking."

SENSE OF COMPETENCE

Are the student masters at what they do? Are they still learning to master things? Alternatively, have they not been able to conquer any particular thing yet? The assumption of this question is that the students know what their skills and abilities are. Related to their knowledge of their strengths and weaknesses, this question essentially asks, "How comfortable do the students feel in using their gifts and talents?" In addition, has the execution of these gifts and talents contributed to their present success? More than eighty percent (83.9%) of the students felt that their present success was due to their sense of competence in their skills and abilities (see Table 4.6).

Table 4.6 Psychological—Competence

		Frequency	Percent	Valid Percent	Cumulative Percent
Valid	Strongly disagree	1	1.6	1.6	1.6
	Undecided	9	14.5	14.5	16.1
	Agree	30	48.4	48.4	64.5
	Strongly agree	22	35.5	35.5	100.0
Total		62	100.0	100.0	

The student from Florida said, "I may be good at some things, but when I'm put on the spot I may not do my best." The student from Virginia, "I don't think that anything can be mastered, but that's my aim." "I am always working towards getting better," he insists. The student from Louisiana believes that self-confidence comes from one's competence. The student from Maryland accepts that there is always room for improvement in mastering his skills and abilities. The student from Georgia expresses, "If you realize your skills and abilities you can exploit it and become better at it." One of the students from California says that he is willing to learn to gain a new skill, but he is not afraid to tell people that he does not know how to do something. The student from Colorado admits he is "unlocking so many different things, but I need more understanding of my skills."

ADJUSTMENT TO RACISM

Overt racism against young black males in this country is still persistent. They are followed in department stores, stopped by the police on highways and are hired for low paying service jobs. What have been the experiences of these young black men? Have the students adjusted racism? If so, were these adjustments temporary, or have they become a survival technique. When asked if the student's present success is due to the adjustments they have made because of racism, the results were mixed. More than half (54.8%) of the students disagreed, strongly disagreed, or were undecided about the effects of racism on them (see Table 4.7).

Table 4.7 Psychological—Adjustments to Racism

		Frequency	Percent	Valid Percent	Cumulative Percent
Valid	Strongly disagree	6	9.7	9.7	9.7
	Disagree	13	21.0	21.0	30.6
	Undecided	15	24.2	24.2	54.8
	Agree	14	22.6	22.6	77.4
	Strongly agree	14	22.6	22.6	100.0
Total		62	100.0	100.0	

The student from Virginia says, "Racism has not been a major issue for me." The student from Louisiana agreed, "I have always worked with black people, been surrounded by black people, I haven't faced racism overtly." The experiences of the student from Maryland are similar to the student from Louisiana. Yet he realizes, "It's against me, regardless, I haven't made adjustments." The student from Georgia also has not faced a lot of racism because of where he lives. "The little racism I have faced, I see it as people being ignorant." One of the students from California says, "Racism doesn't even matter on my ability to be successful in my life." "It's not an issue at all."

The other student from California has been dealing with racism all his life. "I have learned and understood that racism is jealousy and insecurity."

The student from Kansas has had several racist incidents happen to him, including the time a judge would not shake his hand at a debate and forensics tournament, "I just brushed it off." The most memorable event was when his high school guidance counselor tried to push him towards attending a junior college. "I had low test scores, but God's plan was for me to go to college not a juco." The student from Florida has also experienced several racial incidents. He went to an all—white high school, "where I became as competitive as the whites I grew up around," he says. He also had an incident with his guidance counselor that he was able to recall. "I got accepted to several big names schools (Florida, Florida State, Hampton, Howard, and Morehouse), but everyone thought that I got in because I was black. My guidance counselor told me that because of my scores and grades I could go to any college because I was a minority." The student from Colorado proclaims, "I am universal now. I do not take sides anymore. I can identify with both blacks and whites." He used to get picked on by both blacks and whites when he was little, people used to pull his hair on the school bus." He would get upset with both blacks and whites when he was in school. Now he will help anyone, but when push comes to shove, "I will be down with the blacks."

FURTHER DISCUSSION

Furthermore, the students from Florida, Kansas, and Texas added some words of advice on different subjects that had to do with the psychology of young black men that were not covered on the questionnaire, but are important. The student from Florida declares, "There is no limit to what a black male can do, work hard and don't let anything stop you from your goal." The student from Kansas echoed his sentiments, "The only thing that stops you is you." He further states, "No matter how bad someone doesn't want to give you something I believe God will make it available to you." The student from Texas knows "I can't do what whites do; I have to be better than they are and I have to be prepared. I have self-discipline so that I will be a step ahead." The student from Kansas acknowledges, "I'm still young and I still have a lot of wisdom and knowledge to gain, I will always be learning. Death is the conclusion of your identity." The student from Texas points out the fact "race shapes everything in life. Whites will discriminate against you, [but] blacks don't want you to succeed." The student from Florida concludes, "I know who I am; I want to develop myself more. Everyday you're learning something new, the better you feel about yourself the better you'll do and the more you'll want to do." The student from Texas has discovered more about himself since coming to Atlanta. "I'm on the path to graduation, but I have experienced some problems along the way. I'm on a hard path. I'm afraid of failure. The more challenges, the more I'm alone, the more I discover about myself."

PSYCHOLOGICAL VALUES ASSESSMENT

Psychologically, the students who participated in the survey showed positive signs of what is expected of them as men. Yet, while the majority of the respondents surveyed agreed and strongly agreed that they understand what it is to be an African American, the results were mixed among the students who were interviewed. For some, race did not matter, while others needed to understand it more, but none of the students are in denial of who they are. The students feel that they have some degree of control over their lives, yet they realize that there are some things that they do not have control over. They also feel that they knew their strengths and weaknesses. The students understand that they are still learning about themselves and that they have boundaries. The positive self-esteem of the young black males who were surveyed is extremely high. Yet, one of the interviewees was open enough to say that he did not have positive self-esteem. Most of the students feel that they are competent in their skills and abilities and that is why they are successful. However, a good number of them are still working on their skills and abilities in order to master them. Categorically, the respondents did not let racism stop them from being successful. They are almost defiant of racism in their answers, although, some of them have faced racial incidences. Most of them believe that they are the only obstacle to stand in their way of accomplishing their goals.

CONCLUSION

The research on young black males who attend Clark Atlanta University showed that they have high levels of psychological, spiritual and emotional development. The responses of the students fall in line with previous research on young black males. Their positive self-esteem, belief that racism has minimal effect on their achievement and the support that they get from family members in particular were similar to those found in a study by Sedlacek.[31] Similarly, Simms, Knight, and Dawes noticed that personal support was a contributing factor in the academic success of young black males.[32] The young men surveyed are pursuing their goal of obtaining a college degree. They have overcome the negative attitudes and low expectations of some of their teachers.[33] Several of the students did very well academically during the school year that the interviews were conducted. Education was something that was emphasized to the students by their parents. Subsequently, most of the students come from middle to upper class socio—economic backgrounds. Although the educational attainment of their parents was not apart of the survey, the interviewees gave the impression that most of their parents did not have a college education, but they saw the relevance of a college education for their sons.

The young men interviewed have a good conceptual knowledge of manhood. They are not caught up in the "aggressive" behavior that emphasizes sexual promiscuity and violence as noted by Harris.[34] Despite the lack of positive male role models available to young black males, these young men have been able to identify coaches and relatives, in addition to their fathers, to give them some guidance into manhood. The students learned their concept of manhood from the conversations that they had with their fathers or other positive male role models. In addition, the students felt that these men were good examples of manhood in their everyday life. For some of the students the actions of these men, particularly how they handled discipline, were studied carefully.

The students interviewed realize what it means to be African-American. None of them gave the illusion otherwise. Attending a Historically Black University further affirms their cultural identity. Assimilating into American culture was not an idea that they chose to address in the interviews. However, those interviewed showed greater indecision on the question of what it means to be an African-American. Some of the students felt that African-American was just a label, they are aware of the limits of that label, but they refuse to let this label stop them from achieving their goals. Other students realize that being an African-American means that they will have to work harder to achieve their goals.

The students surveyed had high levels of positive self-esteem. More than ninety percent (90.3%) of the students agreed or strongly agreed that their present success is due to their positive self-esteem. Nearly eighty-four percent (83.9%) accredited their present success to the sense of competence they have in their skills and abilities. Franklin and Mizell saw a correlation between self-esteem and upward mobility.[35] Social buffers also contributed to positive self-esteem the researchers also found.[36] It could be inferred that the origin of the positive self-esteem of the students interviewed came through their relationship with their family and friends.

The students interviewed felt confident that they have mastered, or are mastering, some skills and abilities. For many of the young black males who were interviewed, athletics was a primary skill or ability that they have mastered, or are in the process of mastering. For other students public speaking was something they felt in which they were becoming competent. Mizell states that high religious attendance positively affects self-esteem, which in turn leads to higher mastery.[37] The students interviewed did not show high religious attendance based upon their responses to the question on church involvement (#20), but they did allude to the fact that they attended church more when they were in high school than they do now. In addition, the more education young black males have, the more opportunities they will have, thus leading to a greater sense of control over their lives.[38] The students interviewed felt that they did have some degree of control over their lives. They felt that they were responsible for their own decisions. Paying for college was one area over which they knew they did not have control. However, the students realized that their parents were allowing them to have more independence. This independence has forced some of them to grow up and take control of their lives. It can also be implied, based upon Mizell's research, that these students will have more control over their lives as they gain more education.

The majority of the students surveyed do not believe that racism is a factor in their lives. Harris and Majors report, "Many of the attitudes, opinions and beliefs of African-Americans have been shaped by racism, prejudice and discrimination."[39] Although the students interviewed admitted to having experienced racism, they do not believe that it is an obstacle for them as they attempt to obtain their goals.

Several authors, such as Franklin and Mizell, reiterated the significance of a healthy spiritual life and its correlation to a healthy psychological life.

Franklin and Mizell, who do not teach at Christian colleges or universities, endorse the importance of going to church and related spiritual activities in several of their articles. In the next section spirituality is presented as not only a coping mechanism for the survival of young black males in America, but as a necessity to their psychological and emotional well-being, as well as a prerequisite to the longevity of success.

ENDNOTES:

1)   W. F. Sedlacek, "Black Students on White Campuses: 20 Years of Research," Journal of College Student Personnel 28 (1987): 161–166.

2)   Kevin B. Simms, Donice M. Knight, Jr., Katherine L. Dawes, "Institutional Factors that Influence the Academic Success of African-American Men," Journal of Men's Studies 1 (February 1993): 253.

3)   Clyde W. Franklin and C. Andre Mizell, "Some Factors Influencing Success Among African-American Men: A Preliminary Study," Journal of Men's Studies 3 (February 1995): 191.

4)   Ibid.

5)   Ibid.

6)   Gail Elizabeth Wyatt, "Beyond Invisibility of African-American Males: The Effects on Women and Families," Counseling Psychologist 27 (November 1999): 802–809.

7)   Ibid.

8)   Clyde W. Franklin and C. Andre Mizell, "Some Factors Influencing Success Among African-American Men: A Preliminary Study," Journal of Men's Studies 3 (February 1995): 191.

9)   Jay C. Wade, "African-American Fathers and Sons: Social, Historical, and Psychological Considerations," Families in Society 75 (November 1994): 561.

10)   Ibid.

11)   Ibid.

12)   Ibid.

13)   H. Elaine Rodney and Robert Mupier, "Behavioral Differences between African-American Adolescents with Biological Fathers and Those without Biological Fathers in the Home," Journal of Black Studies 30 (September 1999): 45–61

14) D. Brown, R. Hutchinson, W. Valutis, and J. White, "The Effects of Family Structure on Institutionalized Children's Self-Concepts," *Adolescence* 24 (Summer 1989): 303–310.

15) H. Elaine Rodney and Robert Mupier, "Behavioral Differences between African-American Adolescents with Biological Fathers and Those without Biological Fathers in the Home," *Journal of Black Studies* 30 (September 1999): 45–61.

16) Kenneth I. Maton, Freeman A. Hrabowski III, Geoffrey L. Greif, "Preparing the Way: A Qualitative Study on High-Achieving African-American Males and the Role of the Family," *Journal of Community Psychology* 26 (August 1998): 639–668

17) Ibid.

18) "News and Views: Why the Large and Growing Gender Gap in African-American Higher Education?" *Journal of Blacks in Higher Education* (Spring 1998): 34.

19) Gail Elizabeth Wyatt, "Beyond Invisibility of African-American Males: The Effects on Women and Families," *Counseling Psychologist* 27 (November 1999): 802–809.

20) Anderson, C. L. Eaddy, and E. A. Williams, "Psychological Competence: Toward a Theory of Understanding Positive Mental Health among Black-Americans," in *Handbook of Mental Health and Mental Disorders among Black Americans*, ed. D. Ruiz (Westport, CT: Greenwood Press, 1990), 255–271.

21) Shanette M. Harris and Richard Majors, "Cultural Value Differences: Implications for the Experiences of African-American Men," *Journal of Men's Studies* 1 (February 1993): 227

22) Ibid.

23) Ibid.

24) C. Andre Mizell, "African-American Men's Personal Sense of Mastery: The Consequences of the Adolescent Environment, Self-Concept, and Adult Achievement," *Journal of Black Psychology* 25 (May 1999): 210.

25) Ronald L. Taylor, "Black Youth and Psychosocial Development," *Journal of Black Studies* 6 (June 1976): 353.

26) Ibid.

27) Ibid.

28) Shannette M. Harris, "Psychosocial Development and Black Male Masculinity: Implications for Counseling Economically Disadvantaged African-American Male Adolescents," *Journal of Counseling and Development* 73 (January 1995): 279.

29)   Ibid.

30)   Kevin B. Simms, Donice M. Knight, Jr., Katherine L. Dawes, "Institutional Factors that Influence the Academic Success of African-American Men," *Journal of Men's Studies* 1 (February 1993): 253.

31)   W. F. Sedlacek, "Black students on white campuses: 20 years of research," Journal *of College Student Personnel* 28 (1987): 161–166.

32)   Kevin B. Simms, Donice M. Knight, Jr., Katherine L. Dawes, "Institutional Factors that Influence the Academic Success of African-American Men," *Journal of Men's Studies* 1 (February 1993): 253.

33)   Ibid.

34)   Shannette M. Harris, "Psychosocial development and black male masculinity: Implications for counseling economically disadvantaged African-American male adolescents," *Journal of Counseling and Development* 73 (January 1995): 279.

35)   Clyde W. Franklin and C. Andre Mizell, "Some Factors Influencing Success Among African-American Men: A Preliminary Study," Journal *of Men's Studies* 3 (February 1995): 191.

36)   Ibid.

37)   C. Andre Mizell, "African-American Men's Personal Sense of Mastery: The Consequences of the Adolescent Environment, Self-Concept, and Adult Achievement," *Journal of Black Psychology* 25 (May 1999): 210.

38)   Ibid.

39)   Shanette M. Harris and Richard Majors, "Cultural Value Differences: Implications for the Experiences of African-American Men," *Journal of Men's Studies* 1 (February 1993): 227

CHAPTER FIVE
SPIRITUAL VALUES AND YOUNG BLACK MALES

LITERATURE REVIEW

There is a deficient amount of research on spirituality and black males. Available research attempts to show how spirituality affects the success of young black males. Leon Chestang reveals the historical importance of religion to blacks: "This institution serves the psychological purpose of strengthening the individual in the face of his impotence against the social structure and the sociopolitical function for providing an outlet for his talents and abilities, as well as furnishing a focal point for community organization.[1] Robert Staples asserts, "For years the Blacks' belief in religion has served to fortify them against the psychologically destructive forces of racism."[2] Furthermore, Staples affirms that the black church has acted as a mechanism for reducing tension and as a defense against the hostile white world, while giving credence to the cultural heritage of black people, validating their self-worth and providing them with hope for the future.[3]

CHURCH INVOLVEMENT

Herbert H. Toler hypothesizes that "The most effective way to reduce black crime and to strengthen black families may be to return African-American men to their spiritual roots."[4] He further states, "In earlier generations, black men were much more involved in the church and their religious faith bolstered their commitment to families and neighborhoods."[5] Toler examines how the men's ministry at a prominent church in Baltimore has affected the lives of black men. Reconciliation, responsibility, commitment and dedication are a few of the adjectives he uses to describe the effectiveness of this program. The church teaches its men about Africans in the Bible and throughout Christian history. It also offers Bible studies just for men. They teach men how to handle their anger and other issues they have in their lives.[6]

SPIRITUAL DEVELOPMENT

Church provides a positive support structure that may not exist for young black males in any other institutional form. Spiritual role modeling has a big impact on black males. At one church, the pastor has created an environment where men are encouraged to admit their errors and make restitution with no stigma attached. In addition, the pastor teaches each man individually about Africans in the Bible for one hour before they can become members of the church.[7] As the black church is the only solely owned black institution in America, it has the potential to be the place to develop young black males spiritually. The personality of a pastor has a lot to do with attracting young black males to church. Many young black males do not attend church because there are not enough black men in the church to lead them, or they do not like the pastor. It is not a secret that women are the backbone of the black church. Yet, Franklin and Mizell found that "religion was an important ideology for the upwardly mobile [black males]."[8] Black men who are involved in church activities have a degree of power that they may not have elsewhere. Mizell further states that religious involvement provides social support as well.[9] Religious involvement is associated with high self-esteem, self-mastery and positive mental health. These factors all interact to support African-American men's upward social mobility.[10]

SELF-DISCOVERY

Sheldon Nix believes that "sooner or later we are forced by life and by God to confront who we really are and the outcome of that confrontation will determine whether we will become the kind of man God created us to be . . . whether we pass on our lives to the next generation of African-American boys."[11] He states further that successful people focus on principles and purpose.[12] When young black men discover the purpose for which God created them, they see the world in a completely new way. Walter McCray proposes, "Secular black adolescence is destroying generation after generation of precious Black young adults. By the time some Black adolescents reach young adulthood, their lives have already been wasted—body, mind and spirit."[13]

It is the church's responsibility to influence black young adults holistically, but in particular spiritually, so that they will be able to lead the black community.[14] While some young black males are spiritually mature and psychologically healthy, emotionally most young black males have some unresolved issues. This is not to suggest that they are unique in that aspect; however, the way that they deal with these issues has been the cause of many broken male/female relationships, which has brought about an increase in the number of suicides by young black males and produced the large number of homicides that are committed by young black males.

SPIRITUALITY AND YOUNG BLACK MALES

The six questions (#15–20) that refer to spirituality and how it relates to their success are on: their beliefs and values, spiritual disciplines, understanding their spiritual purpose in life, the hope they have in God, the role spirituality has played in their lives and their church involvement. Seventy-five percent of the students agreed or strongly agreed with the first five questions (#15–19) on spirituality. However, there was sharp disagreement on the role of church involvement being a part of their success. A little less than half (47.5%) of the respondents disagreed, strongly disagreed, or were undecided about how church involvement correlated with their present success.

SPIRITUAL BELIEFS AND VALUES

Spiritual beliefs and values are the essence of who we are. What we believe about the world, people, God and ourselves govern who we are and how we act. For many, it is the foundation upon which they live. What one believes determines what one values. If one believes life is precious, then one probably would not attempt to kill someone. Read any college survey, what students value and believe about spiritual things is of great interest to many. What do they believe and why? How does what they believe contribute to their success? Eighty-seven percent (87.1%) believed that their spiritual beliefs and values about life were vital to their present success (see Table 5.1).

Table 5.1 Spirituality—Belief & Values

		Frequency	Percent	Valid Percent	Cumulative Percent
Valid	Strongly disagree	1	1.6	1.6	1.6
	Disagree	2	3.2	3.2	4.8
	Undecided	5	8.1	8.1	12.9
	Agree	22	35.5	35.5	48.4
	Strongly agree	32	51.6	51.6	100.0
Total		62	100.0	100.0	

In response to the question about spiritual beliefs and values as a contributor to one's present success; the student from Maryland believes, "Something has to push you everyday, you got to get up in the morning." The student from Virginia admits, "Without God I haven't accomplished anything. I don't feel I would be successful without him." One of the students from California believes in God, but he discloses, "I'm still trying to map out what is expected of me to be a Christian. I want to decide my spiritual beliefs for myself." The student Colorado has a guiding force. "I am in tune with nature and people, I can relate to people. I have a connection with the spirit world." He began to meditate before a recent boxing match, "I had never studied it before; I just listen to the spirit." While the student from Georgia states, "Basically in order to live a successful life you have to have some sort of morals and beliefs, guidelines to live by." He draws the following parallel: "to ensure a good life living in a dorm you have to rules to ensure safety." He feels his spiritual beliefs and values are those rules. The student from Louisiana puts God first spiritually. "Three times a day I pray at least—while I'm walking, driving. Without God I could be anywhere but where I am." His family goes to church occasionally, but as he grew older, he went to church with his step—dad. "The knowledge I learned at church is greater than any other knowledge. Bible stories show triumph over failure." He trusts the reason is that he does not make the mistakes of other people he is "God—fearing." He understands that God puts people through "tests." He testifies that, "My faith grew a lot, has gotten stronger. I have seen what God has done in my life."

SPIRITUAL DISCIPLINES

Spiritual disciplines help us to realize that what is seen is not the whole story. Whether it is prayer, fasting, or meditation, spiritual disciplines keep us centered on what is important, gives us peace and keep us sane in this fast-paced world. Do the students believe in and or practice any spiritual disciplines? If so, how does this practice contribute to their success? More than three-quarters (77.4%) of the students said that spiritual disciplines, such as prayer, are a reason for their present success (see Table 5.2).

Table 5.2 Spiritual—Disciplines

		Frequency	Percent	Valid Percent	Cumulative Percent
Valid	Strongly disagree	2	3.2	3.2	3.2
	Disagree	1	1.6	1.6	4.8
	Undecided	11	17.7	17.7	22.6
	Agree	21	33.9	33.9	56.5
	Strongly agree	27	43.5	43.5	100.0
Total		62	100.0	100.0	

The student from Florida feels that anything he prays for happens. "I pray my way through any problem I have." The student from Georgia believes "through prayer you can get a lot of questions answered." One of the students from California divulged that he does not pray a lot, however "when I do pray it helps." The student from Virginia has faith that "prayer open doors that otherwise would be closed." He is confident when he exclaims, "You can't be afraid to ask the Lord for anything."

The student from Maryland replies, "I don't discipline myself religiously." He was forced to go to church as a young child, but he does not go to church regularly. Although he still prays at night. The student from Colorado did not grow up in church, but he has some understanding and he prays for guidance and comfort. He disclosed, "The cross—country team wants me to work on it (to pray) some more, I don't know why." He confesses that he does not understand the concept of fasting, but he knows it is something he must do. The other student from California admits, "Spiritual disciplines have not played a major role in his life, like at situations whether they are right or wrong." He believes that spiritual disciplines and morals are complementary. Although he understands prayer and forgiveness, he hates it when people use religion as a "crutch." He utters, "I get mad when people say that they will pray about it and it will be all right."

SPIRITUAL PURPOSE

God gives everyone a purpose to accomplish while they are on this earth, if a person believes in God. For many their purpose remains hidden. Eventually, everyone has to answer the question of his purpose or significance. Have these young black males discovered spiritually why they were put on this earth? How does knowing what your spiritual purpose is contribute to your success? More than three-quarters (75.8%) of the students affirmatively responded understanding their spiritual purpose in life is a reason for their present success (see Table 5.3).

Table 5.3 Spiritual—Spiritual Purpose

		Frequency	Percent	Valid Percent	Cumulative Percent
Valid	Strongly disagree	2	3.2	3.2	3.2
	Disagree	2	3.2	3.2	6.5
	Undecided	11	17.7	17.7	24.2
	Agree	19	30.6	30.6	54.8
	Strongly agree	28	45.2	45.2	100.0
Total		62	100.0	100.0	

The student from Kansas understands his purpose, "the struggle exists in my flesh," he confesses. He admits he has to repent for having sex before marriage, as he sees that it does affect him spiritually. The student from Florida feels he is struggling right now. "God understands our humanness," he believes. However, he discloses "I would not do a lot of things that I am doing right now, like sleeping around with different females." The student from Colorado potentially knows what his spiritual purpose is. "When I read about Che Guevara, Mumia Abu Jamal, I feel connected. I feel I will be the voice of the voiceless. I believe my spirit will lead me there. My spiritual purpose—understanding and hope," he says with confidence. One of the students from California trusts "God put me on earth to do something special, I am pursuing it." The student from Virginia admitted that he does not know what his spiritual purpose in life is. "I am going to keep going until my spiritual purpose hits," he says. The student from Louisiana does not know his spiritual purpose yet either, but until he finds out, he says he is going to "serve God to the best of his ability, ask for forgiveness." The student from Maryland has not thought about his spiritual purpose, "I'm young, I am going to live and experience," while the student from Georgia also confesses that he does not know what his spiritual purpose in life is. "Once you know your purpose you can exploit it, you have some sort of sight," he supposes. The other student from California thinks everybody has a job or a role; everybody has a purpose. "I do not question my spiritual purpose, ying and yang."

HOPE IN GOD

Why do people hope in God? Is it because they are too weak to accomplish certain things on their own, or not intelligent enough? On the contrary, hope in God requires that one give over control of something expecting not to lose it, but to regain it again better than it was before. Alternatively, it could be that one turns it over and may never get it back again. Either way individuals trust that it is for their good, not for their harm. The highest response from the students came when they were questioned about their hope in God as it relates to their current success. More than seventy-five percent (75.8%) strongly agreed with that statement (see Table 5.4).

Table 5.4 Spirituality—Hope in God

		Frequency	Percent	Valid Percent	Cumulative Percent
Valid	Strongly disagree	2	3.2	3.2	3.2
	Disagree	1	1.6	1.6	4.8
	Undecided	2	3.2	3.2	8.1
	Agree	10	16.1	16.1	24.2
	Strongly agree	47	75.8	75.8	100.0
Total		62	100.0	100.0	

"My faith is getting stronger," says the student from Louisiana. "I do not hope, I know God has something magnificent for my life," he declares. The student from Georgia believes "through God you get most of your guidance, if you follow his word. Through God miracles happen." The student from Colorado has faith "I am walking on his path; God is seeing me through it. I have great hope in God." He further maintains, "As soon as you understand God, you understand your purpose." One of the students from California accepts as truth that "God has his back." The other California student asserts that thinking about God is too huge. "If I can pray to God, I know that there is a God, I don't worry about the petty matters," he asserts. The student from Florida acknowledges, "That's where my hope is." He goes on further to say "I depend on God for a job, a house, a wife. So far God has blessed my life." The student from Texas says that he has hope in God, but he divulges, "In the area I struggle with, I have no hope." He admits that hope for what he struggles with "may not happen while he is alive."

ROLE OF SPIRITUALITY

Spirituality concerns the belief in what one cannot see, touch, or control. Religious knowledge is internalized and life decisions are filtered through personal convictions about God. How has spirituality made an impact, if it has, on young black men? More than eighty percent (80.6%) of the students believe that their present success is due to the role that spirituality has played in their lives.

Table 5.5 Spiritual—Role of Spirituality

		Frequency	Percent	Valid Percent	Cumulative Percent
Valid	Strongly disagree	2	3.2	3.2	3.2
	Disagree	2	3.2	3.2	6.5
	Undecided	8	12.9	12.9	19.4
	Agree	21	33.9	33.9	53.2
	Strongly agree	29	46.8	46.8	100.0
Total		62	100.0	100.0	

The student from Kansas says that he was raised as a Christian. His grandmother taught him about God. He testifies, "I always went to church. I pray a lot. I have seen God do things for me." He admitted that he still has room to grow. The student from Florida was also raised as a Christian. His mother taught him about God. He always went to church. "I am dependent on God," he confesses. "Some things I don't want to tell my brothers, but I will tell God," he asserts. He states, "I know a lot about God, but I don't live what I know." He discloses that he is working on it. The student from Texas struggles with the role that spirituality has played in his life. He purports the depth of his spirituality has varied throughout his life. "My struggles have cost me to lose my spiritual fervor. I did not understand why those who were not living the right life were doing well, while I was not doing well." He does not expect things to happen, like "being delivered from a personal struggle." The student from Maryland says that spirituality is a source of energy for him. The student from Colorado agrees. "You have to be connected with nature, if I wasn't connected to the role of spirituality I would be like Jay-Z," he asserts. "No rap music or girlfriend's love can compare," he affirms. The student from Georgia believes, "It is good for everybody to be a spiritual person, have some sort of belief in something, faith that God will come through for us." One of the students from California articulates, "Religious people are ignorant." "Spirituality is bigger than anyone, people like to satisfy what is good for them," he believes.

CHURCH INVOLVEMENT

The church is a body of local believers who come together periodically for worship of God, spiritual instruction, prayer and more. Churches also offer people the opportunity to serve in certain areas and to lead in others. It affords people the opportunity to use their gifts, talents and abilities where they might not be able to use them anywhere else. About half (47.5%) of the respondents to the survey disagreed, strongly disagreed, or were undecided about how church involvement played a part in their present success (see Table 5.6), while the remainder (52.5%) agreed or strongly agreed about the importance of church involvement.

Table 5.6 Spirituality—Church Involvement

		Frequency	Percent	Valid Percent	Cumulative Percent
Valid	Strongly disagree	7	11.3	11.5	11.5
	Disagree	6	9.7	9.8	21.3
	Undecided	16	25.8	26.2	47.5
	Agree	17	27.4	27.9	75.4
	Strongly agree	15	24.2	24.6	100.0
	Total	61	98.4	100.0	
Missing	System	1	1.6		
Total		62	100.0		

The student from Virginia grew up in church, where he learned a lot about faith. However, he discloses "I don't do everything right, I do a lot of things wrong." The student from Louisiana infers that he is not involved in church, "I only benefit from the teaching at church." The student from Maryland is not involved in church, "It's not much of a factor." The student from Georgia trusts the fact that "church helps you not forget how you should live life." The student from Colorado did not grow up in church. "I went to Catholic school and was held back twice," he divulges. "My nature said that I am connected with nature," he believes. "Church is a big fashion show; I did not have the clothes growing up. I can get down on a pillow on the couch and just pray and read the Bible." One of the students from California asserts, "You don't have to go church, just believe." The other student from California contends, "Your success is not due to how many times you attend church." He says, "You can pray, read the Bible; everyone has their own understanding." The student from Kansas sees church as being more business oriented than spiritual. He questions, "The pastor doesn't know who you are, is the pastor teaching the whole truth, I don't believe that there should be as many churches as there are, the church doesn't help you out when you fall down, I'm concerned about how the pastor's teach, speaking in tongues." The student from Texas received a lot guidance in church, but he also saw a lot of crookedness in the church. "I don't look at church as being a holy place," he expresses. The messages in church inspire the student from Florida, but the people in church have had a negative effect on him. "They were not motivating me to grow spiritually," he says.

SPIRITUAL VALUES ASSESSMENT

Overall, the young black males who were surveyed showed high levels of spirituality as it relates to their present success. They believe that their spiritual beliefs and values are one of the reasons why they are successful. The spiritual disciplines that they practice have also played a part in their success. Although many of them said that understanding their spiritual purpose in life was of vital importance, upon further study, many of them did not know what their spiritual purpose was, or that they struggled with it. Their faith in God was essential to their present success. Most of the students think they would not be able to accomplish anything without God. The students also sensed that spirituality has been a factor in their present success. Even though some of them are struggling spiritually, they are conscious of the fact that spirituality is a part of life. Church involvement received mixed reviews from the respondents. Some agreed that the teaching in church was important, while others did not. Most of them are of the opinion that going to church is not a necessity to be a spiritual person. Many of them saw through the façade of many churches. They like to question things and for many of them their questions have not been answered. These young black males are successful in part because they are pursuing their goals to graduate from college. Many of them believe that in order to do that they must rely on God.

CONCLUSION

Significantly more research needs to be done on spirituality and young black males, but also on spirituality and black males in general. It is difficult to draw any further conclusions, other than the ones that have already been drawn, about spirituality and young black males. The research on the topic has focused on church attendance, church involvement and the support network that exists in a church setting that is of benefit to young black males. The results of the research conducted in this study show that the students have good conceptual knowledge of spirituality. The students attribute their present success to their spiritual beliefs and values, hope in God and the overall role spirituality has played in their lives. Many of them are still discovering what their spiritual purpose is; in addition, they are developing spiritual disciplines. However, research also needs to be done on what young black males believe about spiritual things. The young black males surveyed made a clear distinction between spirituality and religiosity. It appears that they had learned many spiritual teachings in church when they were younger and although many of them had retained the spiritual teachings that they learned they do not find that the church is a necessary part of their lives anymore. Because the information on young black males has not touched on spirituality in depth, the research of this thesis has contributed to the body of knowledge on successful young black males. The students believe that without spirituality they would not have accomplished what they have so far in their lives. They see that dependence on God is a necessity to becoming successful black men in America. Some believe that the spiritual principles that they live by have kept them out of legal trouble.

ENDNOTES:

1)   Leon Chestang, "Environmental Influences on Social Functioning: The Black Experience," in *The Diverse Society: Implications for Social Policy*, ed. Pastora San Juan Cafferty and Leon Chestang (Washington, D.C. : NASW, 1976), 72.

2)   Robert Staples, *Introduction to Black Sociology* (New York: McGraw Hill, 1976), 82.

3)   Ibid.

4)   Herbert H Toler, Jr., "Fisher of men: A Baltimore Minister Promotes Black Christian Manhood," *Policy Review* 72 (Spring 1995): 72.

5)   Ibid.

6)   Ibid.

7)   Ibid.

8)   Clyde W. Franklin and C. Andre Mizell, "Some Factors Influencing Success Among African-American Men: A Preliminary Study," *Journal of Men's Studies* 3 (February 1995): 191.

9)   C. Andre Mizell, "African-American Men's Personal Sense of Mastery: The Consequences of the Adolescent Environment, Self-Concept, and Adult Achievement," *Journal of Black Psychology* 25 (May 1999): 210.

10)   Clyde W. Franklin and C. Andre Mizell, "Some Factors Influencing Success Among African-American Men: A Preliminary Study," *Journal of Men's Studies* 3 (February 1995): 191.

11)   Sheldon D. Nix, *Becoming Effective Fathers and Mentors* (Woodbury, NJ: Renaissance Productions, 1996), 29.

12)   Ibid.

13)   Walter A. McCray, *Black Young Adults: How to Reach Them, What to Teach Them* (Black Light Fellowship, 1992), 40.

14)   Ibid, 119.

CHAPTER SIX
CONCLUSION

INTRODUCTION

Based on the results of this research, the young black males who were surveyed and interviewed are proving that the mastery of the emotional, psychological and spiritual dimensions of life contribute to the development of successful young black males. Some of the factors that influence successful young black males are: having a close relationship with their fathers or other positive male role models, having a close relationship with their family, making mature decisions, high self-esteem, race—consciousness, their spiritual beliefs and values and their hope in God.

LIMITATIONS OF STUDY

This study only refers to successful young black males and it is not a comparative study with unsuccessful young black males. The setting of the study is Clark Atlanta University, a Historically Black University in Atlanta, Georgia. There is a void of information on young black males and their emotional life. A definitive study needs to be done on why young black males commit violent crimes, as it is a common emotional response of young black males. More research also needs to be conducted on collegiate black males or young black males in general. Most of the research dealt with those under the age of eighteen or those over the age of twenty-five.

IMPLICATIONS ON THE FIELD OF AFRICAN-AMERICAN STUDIES

Conceptually, the ideals of manhood that the successful young black males interviewed have do not center on "hyper—masculine" behavior, or aggressive, violent behavior that also emphasizes sexual promiscuity. It further agrees with research that successful young black males have a higher degree of self-identity and self-esteem. Further research needs to be done on the feelings of successful young black males and the effects of racism. A better understanding of what young black males believe about spiritual things and how spiritual beliefs have played a role in the development of successful young black males would provide some exploration as to what successful young black males believe about spirituality in comparison to religiosity (church involvement). The results show that further research needs to be conducted to identify the men in the lives of successful young black males that influence them the most. In addition, a more definitive study is necessary to better identify the areas that the family plays a role in the development of successful young black males. What they feel about their family, friends and themselves warrants a major research study to better identify the characteristics of successful young black males.

CURRENT SUCCESS SURVEY*

AGE:_____HOMETOWN:_____
RACE:_____CLASSIFICATION:_____

5 – STRONGLY AGREE   4 – AGREE
3 – UNDECIDED   2 – DISAGREE
1 – STRONGLY DISAGREE

MY PRESENT SUCCESS IS DUE TO:
___ 1. my relationship with my father or other positive male role model.
___ 2. my relationship with my family.
___ 3. my relationship with my friends.
___ 4. my acceptance of responsibility.
___ 5. my attempt to resolve the issues of my life that I struggle with.
___ 6. my maturity based upon the decisions I make.
___ 7. my ability to handle my feelings.
___ 8. my understanding of what is expected of me as a man.
___ 9. my understanding of what it is to be an African American.
___10. the sense of control I have over my life.
___11. my knowledge of my strengths and weaknesses.
___12. my positive self-esteem.
___13. the sense of competence I have in my skills and abilities.
___14. the adjustments I have made because of racism.
___15. my spiritual beliefs and values about life.
___16. the spiritual disciplines that I practice, such as prayer.
___17. my understanding of my spiritual purpose in life.
___18. the hope I have in God.
___19. the role spirituality has played in my life.
___20. my church involvement.

*based on the Generalized Expectancy for Success Scale

Anderson, L., C.L. Eaddy, and E. A. Williams. "Psychological Competence: Toward a Theory of understanding Positive Mental Health Among Black Americans," in *Handbook of Mental Health and Mental Disorders among Black Americans,* ed. D. Ruiz. Westport, CT: Greenwood Press, 1990, 255-271.

Brown, D., R. Hutchison, W. Valutis, and J. White. "The Effects of Family Structure on Institutionalized Children's Self–concepts," *Adolescence* 24 (1989): 303-310.

Chestang, Leon. "Environmental Influences on Social Functioning: The Black Experience," in *The Diverse Society: Implications for Social* Policy, ed. Pastora San Juan Cafferty and Leon Chestang. Washington, D.C.: NASW, 1976, 72.

Franklin, Clyde W., and C. Andre Mizell. "Some Factors Influencing Success among African American Men: A Preliminary Study," *Journal of Men's Studies* 3 (February 1995): 191.

Harris, Shannette M., and Richard Majors. "Cultural Value Differences: Implications for the Experiences of African American Men," *Journal of Men's Studies* 1 (February 1993): 227.

Harris, Shanette M. "Psychological Development and Black Male Masculinity: Implications for Counseling Economically Disadvantage African–American Male Adolescents," *Journal of Counseling and Development* 73 (January 1995): 279.

Hill, Robert. *Strengths of African–American Families.* Lanham, MD: University Press, 1999.

King, Anthony E. O. "Understanding Violence Among Young African–American Males: An Afrocentric Perspective," *Journal of Black Studies* 28, no. 1 (1997): 79-96.

Lynn, David B. *The Father: His Role in Child Development.* Monterey, CA: Brooks/Cole, 1974, 265.

Maton, Kenneth I., Freeman A. Hrabowski III, and Geoffrey L. Greif. "Preparing the Way: A Qualitative Study on High–Achieving African–American Males and the Role of the Family," *Journal of Community Psychology* 26 (August 1998): 639-668.

McCray, Walter A. *Black Young Adults: How to Reach Them, What to Teach Them.* Chicago: Black Light Fellowship, 1992, 8-18.

Mizell, C. Andre. "African–American Men's Personal Sense of Mastery: The Consequences of the Adolescent Environment, Self-Concept, and Adult Achievement," *Journal of Black Psychology* 25 (May 1999): 210.

Nix, Sheldon. *Becoming Effective Fathers and Mentors.* Woodbury, NJ: Renaissance Productions, 1996.

News and Views: Why the Large and Growing Gender Gap in African–American Higher Education," *Journal of Blacks in Higher Education* (Spring 1998): 34.

Roach, Ronald. "Where Are the Black Men on Campus?" *Black Issues in Higher Education* 18, no. 6 (2001): 18-21.

Rodney, H. Elaine, and Robert Mupier. "Behavioral Differences between African–American Adolescents with Biological Fathers and Those without Biological Fathers in the Home," *Journal of Black Studies* 30 (September 1999): 45-61.

Sedlacek, W. F. "Black Students on White Campuses: 20 Years of Research," *Journal of College Student Personnel* 28 (1987): 161-166.

Simms, Kevin B., Donice M. Knight, Jr., Katherine L. Dawes. "Institutional Factors That Influence the Academic Success of African–American Men," *Journal of Men's Studies* 1 (February 1993): 253.

Staples, Robert. *Introduction to Black Sociology.* (New York: McGraw Hill, 1976, 82.

Toler, Jr., Herbert H. "Fisher of men: A Baltimore Minister Promotes Black Christian Manhood," *Policy Review* 72 (Spring 1995): 72.

Wade, Jay C. "African–American Fathers and Sons: Social, Historical, and Psychological Considerations," *Families in Society* 75 (November 1994): 561.

Wyatt, Gail Elizabeth. "Beyond Invisibility of African–American Males: The Effects on Women and Families," *Counseling Psychologist* 27 (November 1999): 802-809.

Yeh, Christine J. "Invisibility and Self-Construal in African–American Men: Implications for training and practice," *Counseling Psychologist* 27 (November 1999): 810-819.

Odell Horne, Jr. is a Residential Counselor at the United Methodist Children's Home in Decatur, Georgia. He holds a Master's Degree in African American Studies from Clark Atlanta University, a Bachelor's Degree in Business Administration from Texas College, and a Certificate in Biblical Studies from Bethel Seminary. He has worked with students through various Student Affairs positions at Clark Atlanta University, as well as working with young adults at Ben Hill United Methodist Church in Atlanta, Georgia. This manuscript is an extension of his Master's Thesis work on young black males.

www.ingramcontent.com/pod-product-compliance
Lightning Source LLC
Chambersburg PA
CBHW021823270326
41932CB00007B/320